Use Your Words

Also by Carol Garhart Mooney

Swinging Pendulums

Theories of Attachment

Theories of Childhood, second edition

Theories of Practice

How Teacher Talk
Helps Children Learn

Carol Garhart Mooney

www.redleafpress.org
800-423-8309

Published by Redleaf Press
10 Yorkton Court
St. Paul, MN 55117
www.redleafpress.org

First edition 2005
Cover design by Amy Kirkpatrick
Interior design by Brian Donahue / bedesign, inc.
Typesetting by Brian Donahue / bedesign, inc.
Typeset in Berkeley Book
Printed in the United States of America

Library of Congress Cataloging-in-Publication Data
Mooney, Carol Garhart.
   Use your words : how teacher talk helps children learn / Carol Garhart
Mooney. — 1st ed.
      p. cm.
   ISBN 978-1-929610-67-9
   1. Teacher-student relationships. 2. Interaction analysis in education. 3.
Communication in education. 4. Oral communication.   I. Title.
   LB1033.M59 2005
   371.102'3—dc22
                                2005012939

Printed on acid-free paper   U15-03

· · ·

This book is dedicated with love and admiration
to the memory of Jay Munson (1938–2005), teacher,
mentor, and dear friend. It was Jay who taught me
to use my words more carefully!

Table of

Contents

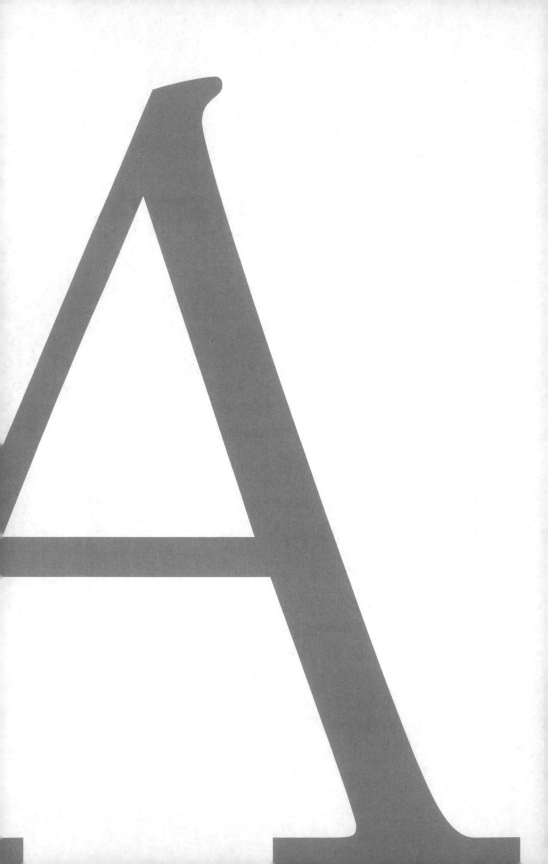

Acknowledgments

• • •

there are so many people who contribute to the successful publication of a book. My thanks and appreciation go first to the professionals at Redleaf Press. My editor, Beth Wallace, is steadfast in making me do my best work and keeps me laughing when the stress is on. Eileen Nelson has been welcoming and supportive from the beginning.

My work is presented in professional form thanks to my longtime friend Marguerite Shanelaris, whose computer and language skills I envy.

My inspiration comes from the teachers who routinely share their classrooms and ideas with me, as well as the children in those rooms who tell me their stories.

The time invested in creating a book is not possible without the support and understanding of special people who spend the book period in a less than reciprocal relationship. In this regard I thank Becky Johnson at Belknap-Merrimack Head Start for her unending patience. I thank the Beths, Ann, Pat, Patrice and Carla and Rich for keeping me going.

Finally, but not at all last, I thank my family: Sean, Johann, Megan, and Caitlin; Brian and Gail; Tom, Angie, and Patty; and most of all Erin, who always carries more than her share.

Introduction

• • •

this is a book about thinking before we speak! Children count on us to make sense of the world for them. Talking is one of the ways we do this. We do it when we play word games with babies. We point to a nose and say *nose*. We point to an ear and say *ear*. Books on child development encourage us to provide babies with many examples of meaningful language, to talk to babies about everything they see, and to describe what we are doing for and with them. Most teachers and parents do a pretty good job at this.

As children grow past babyhood, however, many of us are less effective at communicating with children to support their development of language and thinking. Quick, catchy phrases aren't enough to help children make sense of the world. Yet most early childhood teachers use them to excess. We all care about children but fall short of using language that helps them learn the rules of behavior and expectations of culture and classroom that they need to survive in an increasingly complex world. When we don't adequately explain a word, idea, or concept, we put children at a disadvantage.

· · ·

Language and Learning

We know that children learn to understand language much earlier than they learn to speak. With toddlers we continue to match our use of language to the children's development. We know that children's *receptive language* (the words they understand) is more advanced than their *expressive language* (the words they can say). We know there is a gap between their understanding of a word and their pronunciation of it. The toddler says, "Wawa," and we say, "Yes! Water." We know to set aside the baby talk (sometimes called *motherese*—a high-pitched voice, simple words) that served a sensible social purpose when toddlers were infants.

As children grow, we expect certain developmental milestones, markers like first steps, first words, or using a cup. We know that children will imitate our use of language, will create some language of their own, and will play with rules of language they are just beginning to understand. We know this from research on language acquisition as well as from listening to the children. (For example, see Cazden 1981.)

We know that when Jenny says, "I have dogs at my house," her use of the plural demonstrates her knowledge that she has more than one dog. The same is true when her friend Josh says, "The new shoes hurt my footses." This is also an example of a child *overregularizing* (using language rules he has learned without regard for subtleties or exceptions) as he experiments in the ongoing process of language learning. Most of us are pretty sensible about supporting language learning in these earliest stages.

But as children develop more and more vocabulary, adults in their lives tend to do less and less modeling and purposeful instruction around language. This is a mistake preschool teachers often make. They assume that the need for *deliberate extension* of language (when parents or teachers expand the children's short sentences such as "Mommy here" to *Mommy is here* or "Baby cry" to *The baby is crying*) is not as necessary now that the children are older and know so many words.

Lilian Katz (Katz and Chard 1989, 5) has said, "Teachers throughout the early years tend to overestimate children academically but underestimate them intellectually." Teachers have similar tendencies with language and preschoolers. We forget that children understand words that they don't yet use and use words that they don't yet understand. I am reminded of the child who, when asked how old he was, said, "Can't tell. Got my mittens on!" This was a child who could count to ten or more and could hold up three fingers but didn't yet make the connections among age, numbers, himself, and verbal representation of the three fingers he held up when asked how old he was.

Teacher Jeannette Stone gives a similar example from her early work with Head Start children in the 1960s: "I realized as I said *I'll need you to take turns* that the children had no idea what taking turns meant. So I had to teach them … *First Sherry will use the swing. When she's done Jack can use the swing. This is what we call taking turns*" (Stone 2002). Stone's insight is something many of us lack when talking with young children. We often assume children understand when they don't.

When teachers are not clear, children don't learn, or, worse, they experience confusion or embarrassment because they don't know what to do. Sometimes when children don't know what to do they engage in behaviors that adults find inconvenient or difficult. Yet often adults do not make the connection between the way we speak and the way children act. The purpose of this book is to help make that connection. The way we use our words can truly help children to know what is expected, to understand their world, and to manage within it quite a bit better.

The way teachers use their words can also make their own days less frustrating. Children want to cooperate with us. They want to know what we expect from them. When we take the time to think before we speak, our chances for clarity improve. When we are clearer, children are more cooperative. This makes life easier for all of us and is worth the time and reflection involved.

The ideas presented here are not new. As you read this book, I'm sure you will find yourself saying, "I know that." A trip through most preschools, however, shows us that we all need to remind ourselves to use our words more carefully!

References

• Cazden, Courtney B., ed. 1981. *Language in early childhood education*. Revised edition. Washington, D.C.: National Association for the Education of Young Children.
• Katz, Lilian G., and Sylvia C. Chard. 1989. *Engaging children's minds: The project approach*. Norwood, N.J.: Ablex.
• Stone, Jeannette. 2002. Personal communication.

Chapter 1

Teacher Talk

and Children's Learning

. . .

a colleague recently shared with me one of those "children and language" stories that parents and teachers love to collect. The director was giving a prospective family a tour of her building. In the middle of the tour her assistant interrupted, saying there was an important phone call. The director apologized, saying she had to take the call. Getting down to the child's level, she smiled and said, "This is Nancy. She'll show you our preschool room in the meantime." The child looked alarmed and said

Children
need for us
to continue
to provide
meaning
and defini-
tions for the
thousands of
words we use
every day.
We need to
repeat those
definitions
and extend
the meaning
as children
grow.

politely, "No, thank you. I want to go to the nice time not the mean time!"

These are the stories we all find so charming. *Reader's Digest* offers parents fifty or seventy-five dollars for allowing their inclusion in the monthly family pages. But these stories are far more than cute. They are indicators to us of how easily very young children are confused by our casual use of language. Children need for us to continue to provide meaning and definitions for the thousands of words we use every day. We need to repeat those definitions and extend the meaning as children grow.

Michelle is an Early Head Start teacher who understands the need for all this defining and repetition. All day she talks to and with the children. She asks interesting questions, though her mostly nonverbal children don't answer—*yet!* Each routine, story, and activity is accompanied by many, many words. I listened with delight one day to Michelle's conversation while she was changing a diaper. Timmy was almost two, learning new things every day. Michelle knew that diapering was not one of his favorite things. "I will try to make this quick, Timmy," she said, respectfully. "I know you don't like having to leave your play." As she changed him, she talked about the process, and then elaborated, "Now all I have to do is pull up your pants. Your pants keep your legs warm. I wore my pants today to keep my legs warm. We are wearing pants." The diapering was done. Timmy got down, walked back into the room, looked at me very seriously, and said, "Pants!" This might seem a simple thing, yet I am amazed at the missed opportunities many teachers let pass right by when they could be defining the ordinary but very necessary information about mundane things in our daily lives to which we nonetheless need to put words. Those of us who work with infants and toddlers need to make this a continual approach to teaching the very young.

. . .

What Is at Stake?

In the example about the "mean time" not much damage was done. But as I write these words in February of one of New England's worst winters in years, I think of three-and-a-half-year-old Brianna clutching her snowsuit. When I entered the room yesterday, she was sitting in her cubby, sobbing and kicking. The two teachers were upset and puzzled by this unexpected behavior. As I observed, the volunteer grandmother took over trying to calm Brianna, and the two teachers continued their debate about taking children outside.

The first teacher said, "So many kids are getting sick. They need fresh air."

Her colleague responded, "But with snow this deep, how can we watch them? They'll disappear!"

It didn't take long for me to connect Brianna's sobbing (she usually loved outdoor play) with the murky notion that she could disappear and never be found!

This is something demanding more thought from all of us. Every early childhood textbook cautions beginning teachers against talking about the children as if they were not listening and watching adults' every move. Yet it's easy to do this without giving any thought to our words or their consequences. All of these phrases have been spoken over children's heads in my workplace in the past month:

- "Do you think she needs the nebulizer?"
- "She feels hot. Should we call the nurse?"
- "He seems so tired. I hope we don't have a hard time settling him for nap."
- "Did he have mittens when he arrived? I can't find any in his cubby."
- "Watch her—she's been biting Heather every chance she gets!"

I work with NAEYC (National Association for the Education of Young Children)–accredited programs in which well-educated teachers care deeply about children and teaching. None of the above statements are particularly unprofessional, yet each violates the basic premise that we should not talk about children in their presence as if they are not there. Imagine yourself in the position of a small child listening to powerful adults discuss you this way over your head. Would you feel afraid if you heard them discussing your difficulty breathing? If you heard that you might have a hard time settling down to sleep, how would that affect you when you lay down on your mat? Would hearing that you've been biting every chance you got make you feel more or less in control, more or less frustration? How do these phrases make it easier or harder for teachers and children to manage the common classroom challenges they represent?

Why does this happen? Adults have a much more sophisticated understanding of the world than children do. They have the capacity for abstract thinking, while preschoolers' thinking is still very literal. Adults whose first language is English have internalized many English idioms and shortcuts that are very confusing to young children and to children or adults whose home language is not English. Here are some more examples:

- I'm not telling her. I got burned last month for that.
- We've got problems now—the computer crashed!
- Right! That will happen when pigs fly!
- I think she got up on the wrong side of the bed.

Think for a moment about the images these common statements conjure up to a three- or four-year-old who takes every statement at face value. To a preschooler, the word *crash* describes something you do on bikes or in a car accident. It is a forceful physical event accompanied by noise, broken glass, and crumpled metal, or your friend crying because you ran your bike over her toe. What meaning can this young child make of a "computer crash"?

If we go back to Brianna screaming in her cubby, there are many questions for a concerned teacher to ask:

- Is she feeling threatened because we don't seem to know what to do and are arguing about it in front of her?
- What is her understanding of *disappear*?
- Am I mistaking fear for misbehavior or lack of cooperation?
- What has she seen or heard on TV or radio about the disappearance of a child or parent?

- Have I tried to console her or said, "You're okay, Brianna," without asking why she's upset?

Brianna's teachers were focused on two things: making the decision about outdoor play and trying to get a squirming, screaming little one into a snowsuit. Although both are part of a day's work with young children, these teachers were missing their point for being involved in this work—to help children understand the world around them.

What could they have done instead? The conversation about when or whether to go outside because of the temperature and depth of snow might have taken place early in the morning before the children arrived. This is part of the daily planning process. Before children arrive, teachers can speak together in a brief or abbreviated way that they understand but young children might not. This avoids confusion for children.

If that didn't happen, the teachers might have thought about Brianna's unusual reaction

> Adults have a much more sophisticated understanding of the world than children do. They have the capacity for abstract thinking, while preschoolers' thinking is still very literal.

and tried to figure out what it meant. Since they knew her well, they knew she loved her time in the outdoors.

If she's not too upset to talk, the first thing to do would be to ask Brianna, "What is this about?" That might have ended the situation. I remember walking in on little Evan in tears early in the morning and saying, "Are you missing Mom this morning?" Quickly he rubbed his eyes and said, "Nope. Cook let me help do onions for our soup, and they gotted in my eyes!" So often adults make wrong assumptions about what children are think-ing and feeling. If teachers take the time to investigate the meaning of children's behavior by asking them about it, children are often able to tell them what's going on.

If teachers say something foolish or simply thought-less, it is easy enough to backtrack. In this situation, the teachers could have said something like, "I was being silly, Brianna. We won't disappear. It's just that the snow is very, very deep. Chris and I were just talking about being able to watch all of you as you play in that deep, deep snow. Can I help you with your snowsuit? I know how you love to play in the snow."

I observed an excellent example of this kind of language clarification recently in an Early Head Start classroom in which all of the children are just begin-ning to use language and understand consequences. An assistant teacher made the classic mistake of saying to a young two-year-old, "Would you like to join us for lunch now, Josh?" Her lead teacher, modeling well for both the child and the assistant teacher, scooped him up and said tactfully, "We confused you, Josh. That sounded like a choice, but it's time to eat. I'll help you find your seat." He smiled, settled, and sipped his soup.

This example shows how easily thoughtless teacher talk confuses children, the kind of regrouping we can do when we know it has happened, and the child's cooperative response to clear directions and knowing what is expected of him.

• • •

What's in This Book?

When we talk with young children we use language for a variety of reasons. It is our hope to increase the child's vocabulary, model the correct pronunciation, and make meaning and provide contexts for the thousands of words we use every day. Four specific functions of language that teachers frequently have in mind when communicating with children are addressed in the next four chapters. These are:

- to provide direction or give instructions
- to correct and redirect behavior
- to develop concepts and skills
- to discuss classroom or family life

Throughout the day teachers need to inform children about what's coming next or tell them what's expected of them. When teachers are not precise, their vague directions confuse children and can lead to misunderstandings. Chapter 2 will focus on the opportunities we have to help children understand what we mean when we give directions, show why clarity is important, and offer some typical examples that arise in most preschool rooms.

> It is our hope to increase the child's vocabulary, model the correct pronunciation, and make meaning and provide contexts for the thousands of words we use every day.

Correcting and redirecting behavior is one of the most important functions of language in the early years and also one of the most frequently misused! We do not mean to give the wrong messages to young children, but we frequently do. This will be discussed at length in Chapter 3.

As teachers of young children we are usually very excited about sharing concepts and assisting children in developing necessary skills. Too often, however, we think of skill development in too narrow a way. Many teachers assume that concept development means such things as short and tall, colors, shapes, letters, numbers, sink and float. More critical to school and life readiness are practical skills such as Jeannette Stone's example of taking turns (see page 4). We must teach the typical academic skills of the preschool years. The social and practical skills children need to understand and function in the world around them are equally critical to their future academic success. Chapter 4 will discuss language teachers can use to support children's development of knowledge.

Discussing classroom and family events provides teachers with many opportunities to expand both language and understanding for children. The United States is an increasingly diverse country. Teachers are serving children from many countries, family situations, and class backgrounds. Americans are tremendously diverse in the ways they live at home and the things they think are important. It is not uncommon for *ethnocentrism* (thinking the way one culture or class or family does things is the only or the best way) to affect teachers' conversations and approaches with children and families. This calls for us to think before we speak.

The complexity of discussing classroom events and family stories will be investigated in Chapter 5, which includes tips to help teachers develop a repertoire of skills for navigating turbulent waters involving differing family and cultural values.

• • •

Basic Guidelines

Where do we start? The following chapters will give you a variety of skills and strategies to use when talking with children in the four main contexts. Here are some basic guidelines that will help you begin to think more clearly about your conversations with children in the classroom.

- **Make sure you have the child's attention before you begin to speak.** This is easier if you are close to the child and down on her level. A gentle hand on her arm might help, too, depending on the child and the situation.

- **Always get down to a child's level when talking to her.** If sitting on the floor or squatting is uncomfortable for you, try keeping a chair handy.

- **Remember that body language, tone of voice, and facial expression affect the message you deliver.** The same phrase can be reassuring or threatening depending on how you say it. Words matter. Your expression and tone of voice matter just as much, and sometimes more.

- **Use simple words and short sentences.** Avoid idioms and shortcuts. Try to say exactly what you mean as clearly as possible. If you do use idioms, watch for signs of confusion, and be prepared to explain them.

- **Don't be wishy-washy.** If you mean no, say it. If you say no, mean it!

- **Don't ask a question or offer a choice when there isn't one.** Let children know clearly what you need from them. In particular, avoid using "okay?" at the end of directives, as in "It's clean-up time, okay?"

- **Don't ask questions to which you already know the answer.** This applies to managing behavior as well as concept development. Don't ask a child, "Is that the way we treat our friends?" You already know that pushing another child is not a good way to treat him, but a young child doesn't yet. Likewise, there are better ways to develop children's thinking skills than to ask them questions about numbers and colors and letters to which you already know the answer.

- **If you must interrupt children, remember they deserve the same courtesy adults expect.** Say something like "Excuse me, I need you in the book corner now, please." Teach *please*, *thank you*, *I'm sorry*, *you're welcome*, and other niceties by your own modeling rather than prodding with that old "What do you say?"

- **Use praise in moderation and only when it is sincere and truly called for.** When you are praising a child, be specific—for example, instead of just saying, "Good job!" follow it with the appreciated behavior: "Good job picking up the blocks." Better yet, avoid praise altogether, and comment on or thank the child for the work she did. For example, "You did a lot of work picking up those blocks," or "Thank you for picking up so many blocks. Look how much space there is now!"

. . .

Discussion Questions

 Can you think of a time when a child was trying to tell you something important but you
missed it because you focused on the wrong
thing? What clues did the child give you that might
have helped? What questions might you have asked
to get at the child's concerns?

 Why do you think teachers often avoid conversations with children that are difficult or
controversial? What difficult topics have come up
when you are working with children? How might you
handle them in the future?

 When do you tend to ask children questions
that you already know the answer to? What
is your purpose when you find yourself doing
this—to manage behavior? to instruct? to find out
what a child knows? How could you accomplish your
purpose in a different way?

Chapter 2

Giving Direction
and Instructions

• • •

throughout the day in early childhood classrooms teachers need to give children direction and instructions. How and when this is
accomplished greatly affects the growth of
both children's understanding and language skills. When
teachers are vague, use catchphrases, or imply information rather than stating it explicitly, children are apt to be
confused. Confused children may be anxious or rebel-
lious. They may comply to the best of their ability silently
or resist instruction. In either case, they are not learning
what they could be, and their feelings may well get in the
way of their ability to take in more information, creating

a negative cycle that can affect children into their elementary school years and beyond.

One area in which many of us seem to be more vague than usual is when we provide children access to creative activities. This probably goes back to some of the old "let children blossom" philosophy, which avoided teacher directions for almost anything. When presenting creative art activities to children, we have all been taught not to draw pictures for children and not to present teacher-made models for the product of the art activity. This is appropriate, but unfortunately many times the use of materials needs to be clearly explained to children, or the consequences can be dire. I am reminded of an art activity involving "spatter painting." The teacher involved was excited about this activity, which involved taping a cutout of an autumn leaf onto a piece of easel paper and letting the children spatter red, yellow, and orange paint around it to create a background. She demonstrated for the children how to hold the brush and flick it a little, sending a spatter of paint across the paper. This was a good start. She both told the children and showed them what to do. In this case, however, knowing how children love process and experimentation, the teacher should have said a few words about what *not* to do. Thinking she had her bases covered, she left the children at the easel and moved on to other areas. The loud giggling and shouts drew her back to the easels to find that children were spattering the walls, the floor, and each other. This inexperienced teacher then understandably thought the children were misbehaving, when clearly they were simply deeply engaged in the activity she had provided for them without giving enough clear instruction about the process!

The answer is not to avoid giving direction or instruction—that would be impossible. The answer is twofold: you can pay attention to being clear, direct, and precise in your instructions and directions to children, and you can assume that children who did not follow directions did not understand them and go from there.

Here is a story of a very similar activity that could have gone awry but did not because the teacher recognized the possibility for too much experimentation and carefully explained the activity to the children. Lori had seen an activity she thought the children would find interesting. It was a kind of texture painting created by filling a piece of panty hose with popcorn kernels, tying a knot, and then dabbing, rolling, or dotting the paint onto the paper. I was fascinated but also impressed as Lori took time to explain that the hose pieces were not to be swung in the air, used any place except on the paper, untied, or used in any way other than as a paint applicator. "Does everyone know what I need you to do?" she asked. It's such a simple sentence—"Does everyone know what I need you to do?"—yet it can clarify so much. The activity went quite well. Lori observed, however, that the materials were almost as interesting to the children as the painting activity. The children had perhaps never played with panty hose before and found the texture, stretchability, and feel of popcorn inside to be quite engaging. Observing carefully, she was able to keep the children on task with the painting while acknowledging their fascination with this particular paint applicator. "I'll fill some more while you finish painting," she said. "Then when we go outside, we'll see what else you can do with them. There is more space outside, and we won't use paint!" The children were delighted. Outside, they stretched, pulled, played catch, had contests throwing them up in the air and across the field. This story illustrates a teacher listening to the children, following their lead, yet preventing mess, harm, or out-of-control responses to what truly was an interesting creative activity. Considering all of that potential for experimentation and learning, she took the materials to another place and allowed children to use them in another way that the children also loved. Lori understood that the four-year-olds were bound to swing the materials around inside, spattering the walls and each other, if she handed them to the children without adequate discussion of how to use them. She understood that it was her job, not the children's, to set the boundaries for the use of the materials.

• • •

Giving Specific Direction

One of the primary goals during preschool is to help children learn to follow directions. Clarity is important when teaching children to follow directions, so many teachers offer first a simple, one-step direction and then advance in complexity as a child's understanding increases. Still, there are times when we assume the child is not complying when the actual problem is in the way we phrase the direction.

Think about the times during the day when you need to give children direction. You may need them to sit quietly for a circle time or a story; you may need them to line up to go to the bathroom or outside; you may need them to approach new materials in a certain way. Whatever the situation, the more specific your directions, the more successful you and the children are likely to be. Unfortunately, many of the common directives teachers give children—the things we say without even thinking about it—are not specific enough for children to understand. In addition, many teachers rely on abstract concepts and social norms that children have not had the experience to develop.

For example, have you ever heard a teacher ask children to "sit nicely"? These words are vague and mean different things to different children and families. In addition, "nice" is an abstract concept. Young children are literal thinkers, and they need lots of time, many experiences, and probably some direct instruction to internalize what an abstract word like *nice*, *good*, *cooperative*, *friendly*, or *kind* means. When giving young children directions, be brief and specific: "Sit on your bottom, and don't touch anyone else. Please be quiet so everyone can hear the story and see the pictures."

Here are some of the phrases teachers often use with children. I'm sure you've heard several of them in the last twenty-four hours!

- Be kind.
- Be cooperative.
- Be polite.
- Quiet down.
- Walking feet.
- Listening ears.
- Inside voices.
- Eyes on me.
- Be careful.
- Be safe.
- Take your seat.

- Five more minutes.
- Use your words.

Without explanation, none of these phrases have meaning for children. Even if we have explained once or twice, children need repetition to learn. For example, "That's not polite" doesn't help Jeffrey, who just ate from the serving spoon and put it back in the bowl. Even if it's positively phrased—for example, "We need manners at the table"—the direction doesn't help Jeffrey know what the expectation is and how he can meet it. However, if a teacher says something like "Remember, Jeffrey, the big spoon is for serving. We only use it to put food on our plate, and then put it back in the bowl for others to use," she is teaching Jeffrey entry-level table manners that he can understand. She will probably have to repeat the lesson several times before Jeffrey really grasps the concept, and he may well need more practice after that to get it right all the time, but her specific words have started the process by giving Jeffrey the clear direction he needs.

> **Young children are literal thinkers, and they need lots of time, many experiences, and probably some direct instruction to internalize what an abstract word like *nice, good, cooperative, friendly,* or *kind* means. When giving young children directions, be brief and specific.**

Teachers often assume children understand basic concepts when they don't. Three- and four-year-olds are literal thinkers. Without making too light of a very serious issue in our use of language with young children, one might envision a child thinking, "Take my seat where?" or "How do I put my eyes on her, and I don't think I want to!" Many three- and four-year-olds haven't any notion yet of "fiveness," so five more minutes or even five more orange slices is more likely to increase confusion rather than clarity.

Many children come to us without knowing how to cut with scissors, use a glue container, pour from a pitcher, or pedal a tricycle. Teachers think of these skills at the beginning of the year when they assess children's competence. At the same time, teachers frequently assume that children know what an "inside voice" is or what it means to cooperate, share, clean up, wash up, or do myriad other simple tasks in daily living. In order to help children understand both our words and the routines in their day, we need to explain clearly what we are saying and why. "It's clean-up time" can be clarified with one more simple sentence: "That means everything needs to be put back in its place," or "Playtime is over—we need to put our things away."

If we use a variety of sentences each week to say the same thing, we are helping children to put the same meaning on a variety of words. There is a difference between using many words to provide meaning and using too many words to define a simple idea for a child. We have all heard the ancient story of the small child who got a long discussion of sex education in response to the question "Where did I come from?" when all he wanted to know was his place of birth. This is not what is being recommended here. Instead, I am suggesting that teachers be conscious of making the kind of clarifying statements that expand children's understanding of the world around them.

If we use a variety of sentences each week to say the same thing, we are helping children to put the same meaning on a variety of words.

How does this all play out in real classrooms? Here's a story to show you, from last week's routine visit to one of the programs I work with. I'd only been in the building a few minutes when I heard a teacher say loudly, "I need to hear silence!" I saw a puzzled look on the face of a three-year-old. I could almost hear him thinking, "How do you *hear* silence?"

I continued down the hall, pausing outside the preschool room. The teacher had gathered the children for a group time. "I'll begin the story when everyone is sitting nicely!" she said. The children continued to wiggle and squirm. The teacher became increasingly agitated. Finally her assistant said, "C'mon, kids, we need to crisscross applesauce here." With this more specific information most children quickly shifted to sitting with their legs crossed. However, I also noticed that two children had no idea what "crisscross applesauce" meant.

The teacher began her group time with the story *Green Eggs and Ham*. As usual, the children had comments right off the bat.

"There aren't really no green eggs."

"Are too, like you get in your Easter basket."

"Those aren't real eggs."

"Are too." (Louder.)

"No!" (Louder still.)

Here the teacher interrupted the discussion, saying, "Inside voices." The children ignored her, and her own inside voice got louder. "Inside voices!" she asserted loudly. "We need to get back to our story!" The children settled down again, but several of them were clearly still thinking about the question of green eggs and whether they really exist!

At the end of the story the teacher asked, "What happened?"

The children said in unison, "He liked the green eggs and ham."

The teacher beamed and said, "So you see we should always have a no-thank-you bite because we have to try things. We can't say we don't like something if we never tried it."

At this point my own inside voices were speaking to me. Here's what they said:

- Is this teacher's agenda to get the children to eat more at mealtimes?
- What is a no-thank-you bite? If you say, "No, thank you," doesn't that mean you don't want any? Why the jump to no-thank-you bites from a Seuss story the children love?
- Do the children know what the teacher means when she says "inside voices"? (I saw no evidence that they did.)
- Why say "crisscross applesauce" if what you mean is "Sit on your bottom, and cross your legs"?

In Chapter 4 we'll talk about the learning that was missed in this situation when the teacher didn't follow up on the children's disagreements about green eggs. For now, though, think about the difference between the directions this teacher gave the children and the behavior she wanted from them. Can you come up with more specific ways to phrase the directions? How might this story time have been different if the teacher had asked for what she wanted? What would have been the effect on the children's learning about the behavior expected of them during story time, about language, and about the content of the book?

Here's another example. What did the teacher in this story do that worked better?

Teachers in New England have a long winter to contend with. Cold and snowy weather places severe constraints on the high energy of preschoolers in programs with little indoor space for running, biking, throwing, and so on. When one fortunate program had a building addition with a large gross motor room, it took time to understand how to use it!

When Kathy took her group to the room for the first time, everyone was excited. Before the children left the classroom, she had talked about safety, taking turns, and riding trikes in the same direction. When she thought the bases were covered, the group set off for the long walk down the hall, down the stairs, and into the big room. The children shrieked with excitement, raced for the trikes, pushed, and shoved, and the riders were the "fittest" who survived the mad dash! Kathy was discouraged. "Should I have waited to get downstairs before talking about safety?" she asked. "How do I do the trikes when there are only eight of them and seventeen children? The children just race for them before I get the chance to do anything!"

Kathy and I talked about the fact that her reaction to this had been one of frustration and helplessness. She did not say, "Stop right there!" or "Absolutely not!" or call the children to an immediate group time to say, "This was not our plan!" Until we talked about it, it had not occurred to her that she really hadn't done anything to redirect the group. She had assumed it was too late. As teachers we are always able to use our adult position to change the course of events when we think it is necessary. We can stop a story time, art activity, or game and say, "This isn't working." We don't have to forge on when things are not going well simply because that was the plan.

This was welcome information for this teacher. Kathy spent time thinking about entrance strategies. Her ideas were good ones. She established a "rental car" booth with tickets, a cash register, and even a gas pump. The rental tickets had children's names on them. The first eight were distributed at group time, upstairs. These children knew that this gave them "driving rights" as soon as they got to the gross motor room. The addition of the gas pump, rent-a-car business, and cash register drew in the remaining children so that now the trikes were not the only point of interest. Kathy made stop signs and one-way signs and talked about following directions when you drive. With a little bit of extra effort and a whole lot of thought, she transformed a chaotic race into meaningful learning and play time that everyone, including the teacher, was able to enjoy!

• • •

Providing Instruction

One of the most important jobs that are part of teaching young children is helping them make sense of the people and relationships around them, helping them to learn to be with one another in groups. One way that teachers can do this is by giving children instruction and practice in talking with others about their needs and wants and solving problems together. Unfortunately, often teachers fall back on "Use your words" as an all-purpose tool. For young children, who don't yet have a lot of experience with words or with relationships, this catch-phrase is inadequate. It doesn't give them enough specific information to solve their problems. They don't know which words to use or how or what to do when the first set of words doesn't work.

Many times teachers experience one child's hitting another as a behavior problem, when it's really the result of a lack of clear instruction. When a teacher says to a child, "Is that how we treat our friends?" she is setting both the child and herself up for more confusion. Such a question violates one of the most basic guidelines for talking with young children: don't ask the question if you already know the answer. The teacher knows that pushing someone when you want her to get out of the way is not the way we treat our friends—or even people who aren't our friends. However, preschool children, relatively new to the planet, do not necessarily know this. Even if they know it in theory, they often don't know what to do instead or don't have experience with problem solving. It is our job to teach them. Teachers must take seriously the task of giving children tools for managing their day-to-day interactions with others.

A better response to a child's pushing a friend out of the way might be to say something like "Adam, tell Sam she is in your way. Ask her to move," or "Sam, tell Adam you don't like it when he pushes you. Ask him what he wants." This clarifies for both children that pushing isn't the answer. It gives both of them the opportunity to use language to tell others how they feel or what they need, and it offers them the specific words to use. These life skills are essential to all of us. If three-year-old Sam is in the way of three-year-old Adam's trike, Adam does not think that it might be seen as antisocial to shove Sam out of the way. Adam has a goal: getting the trike (he might be learning from experience that they go fast once vacated!). Someone needs to help him to learn that we cannot just shove others out of our way when we want something, but we cannot expect children to know this before they have had both instruction and practice in ways of getting what they need or want that work in groups of children.

Mistaking behavioral issues for educational ones will be discussed, at length, in Chapter 3, but for now the lesson is that children need to be taught explicitly how to use language to get what they need and given lots and lots of practice before we expect them to get it right.

Children need to be taught explicitly how to use language to get what they need and given lots and lots of practice before we expect them to get it right.

Mandy plans and teaches at an Early Head Start socialization, a group time and interaction for parents and children who usually have their educational time at home but get together one day a week. She went to her supervisor requesting additional staff because she felt the time was too chaotic. She had children ages six weeks to two years and their parents in her group. The classroom was quite large and could easily accommodate the numbers, but Mandy felt the babies were at risk because the older children were too active.

Her supervisor went to observe and found Mandy had fallen into the typical dilemma of mistaking behavioral concerns for educational ones. Mandy's planning had involved activities and materials but not working with the children to help them understand what the rules of the classroom were. Since the children were very young and came only once a week, Mandy assumed that it was not possible to teach them expectations or approaches. She was also feeling a little uncertain about directing the children when their parents were present.

Her supervisor was able to work with her on modeling adult behavior for the parents. Mandy started by talking to the toddlers, a couple at a time. She talked about babies. "Babies can't get out of our way," she said, "because they don't walk yet." She went on briefly to tell the toddlers that they were the ones who had to watch where they were going. She was surprised how quickly the children developed a feeling of "protecting" the babies. Mandy realized that she had not been using enough language with the children. Children this young need things repeated and repeated and repeated. She continued to use "Watch for the babies" in her own language to the children on a very frequent basis. She gave more specific directions to the toddlers each time she introduced an activity, saying things like these:

- "The trikes need to stay in this part of the room. Trikes are not allowed on the rug."
- "The playdough needs to stay on the table."
- "Blocks are for building. Bean bags are for throwing."

Mandy also changed her room arrangement, using furniture to create barriers. She created sitting areas where parents and babies could be on the floor out of the way of toddler activity. All of these strategies made a huge difference to the day. It was an extra bonus for Mandy when she realized how quickly the parents had followed her lead. "Watch for the babies," parents were saying! And then one day two-year-old Trevor put his hand on eighteen-month-old Amelia's arm when she was poised to throw a bean bag. All he said was, "Baby!"

• • •

Asking Questions

Lack of thoughtful questioning creates many classroom problems. A very common example is using a question that implies choice when there really isn't one. We all seem to do it. Here are some examples:

- Would you like to clean that up, please?
- Would you like to go outside now?
- Would you like a no-thank-you taste?

- Would you like to share the swing now?
- Don't you think you should hold onto the handle?

In each of these cases the adult is expecting compliance but not making that clear. We decrease frustration for children in a tough spot if we avoid using questions that imply choice when there is none. Better to use phrases like these when there is no choice:

- Do you need some help to clean up that spilled milk?
- We are going outside now. You put on your coat, or I'll help you.
- I need to put a few green beans on your plate. If you don't want them, don't eat them.
- I'll set the timer, and when it dings, it will be time for Cal to have a turn on the swing.
- If you don't hold onto the handle, you need to get off the trampoline. I'll help you find something safe to do.

Children are confused and sometimes resentful when we use language in a way that is unclear or manipulative. Being clear when we need them to comply with a directive (and offering them real choices when we can) removes that emotional overlay and makes the job of getting through the day much easier.

Here are some guidelines for providing clear direction and instruction:

- **Be clear and specific.** Don't use catchphrases or abstract concepts without providing explanations.

- **Be concrete.** Remember that children are literal thinkers.

- **Be direct.** Tell children what your expectations are simply and clearly.

- **Use statements, not questions, when you expect children to comply.** Don't offer a choice when there isn't one.

- **Make directions and instructions simple.** Start with one step at a time until you are sure that children have mastered that.

- **Give children specific words to use in conflict.**

- **Give children lots of practice and support in resolving conflicts.**

- **If children don't comply, assume first that they don't understand, and rephrase.**

• • •
Discussion Questions

1. Why do you think teachers are so hesitant to provide children with direct instruction?

2. Share an example of a time when you gave vague instructions that resulted in an activity going poorly. What happened? What could you have done instead?

3. What are some of the things that prevent us from stating our expectations clearly? What can we do to remove some of these barriers to clear communications with children?

Chapter 3

Correcting
Behavior

• • •

the most sought-after topic in early childhood education is behavior guidance. The subject is the source of book after book and technique after technique. Teachers never seem to get enough. Yet most classrooms I visit are still characterized by daily struggles with children's behaviors. Most teachers claim it has never been harder to manage children's daily interactions with the environment and each other. One of the things that nourish this ever-present challenge is the tendency to mistake developmental or educational issues for behavioral problems. Too often teachers think of children as misbehaving when they are simply behaving as best they can with the information available to them.

Understanding development is critical to setting reasonable expectations for children's behaviors. Being patient is more important than we often realize. It is sometimes helpful to compare children's social skill behaviors to their cognitive or physical behaviors. When we are reading to little ones, we don't expect them to retell the story word for word. We get excited when they learn to turn a page or recognize a familiar object in an illustration. When the baby learns to walk, we are excited by each shaky step. We are helpful and encouraging as the toddler teeters and falls again and again. Yet when it comes to hitting and biting, kicking and grabbing—the baby steps of pro-social behaviors—we get terribly impatient. We use words like *so hard*, *difficult*, *frequent*. Few teachers would refer to a child's initial experience with paper books as "ripping too frequently," or call a child's repeated attempts at standing "difficult"! In those other areas of development we tend to be far more patient, far less frustrated, and far less worried about a timeline. There are reasons for this, of course. Our job is to keep children safe, and hitting, kicking, biting, shoving, and grabbing put everyone at risk. But often the way we approach these challenging situations puts everyone in a riskier place than they were already in.

Lilian Katz (1977) says, "Young children have to have adults who accept the authority that is theirs by virtue of their greater experience, knowledge, and wisdom. This proposition is based on the assumption that neither as parents nor as educators are we caught between the extremes of authoritarianism and permissiveness." Nearly three decades later it seems we are still caught in our uncertainty. Most teachers I know who are struggling with how to talk to children about behavior are full of ambivalence. They want to be effective and help children learn positive strategies for interacting, but they don't want to take charge. They don't want to accept the authority that is theirs.

It was late March in New Hampshire when I visited Corinne's classroom. Teachers had gathered umbrellas for use under the melting icicles along the edges of the building. Children wore rain jackets and boots and were enjoying the melting of snow and ice. During a twenty-five-minute outdoor play time, it did not take long for problems like running with umbrellas, climbing with umbrellas, and using umbrellas as weapons to surface. Corinne's dilemma was complicated because she had not given specific directions and boundaries for the use of the umbrellas prior to using them. During that brief period of time I heard her tell Hayley four times, "Umbrellas are not allowed on the climbing structure." This statement was ignored four times by Hayley, who might not have had any idea that Corinne was trying to tell her to get down but didn't actually tell her that!

What exactly were the problems here?

- Corinne did not give specific directions for use of materials *in advance*.
- She was not at all clear in her expectations. (For example, saying that umbrellas cannot go up a climbing structure is unclear to children.)
- Corinne delivered an opinion and thought she had given a directive. (A directive would have been: "Get down. That's not safe.")
- Corinne did not keep children safe. (Hayley was in a dangerous position, and Corinne should have stopped it with a statement like "You may climb *or* play with the umbrella but not both. You make a choice, or I'll need to help you.")
- Corinne did not follow through to remove Hayley from the climbing structure. She kept saying, "Umbrellas are not allowed on the climbing structure," but she allowed it to continue.

A related point to remember here is that if you give a child a directive several times and the child finally follows it, it is not appropriate for you to say, "Good job getting down!" It is not a "good job" to ignore directions four or five times. It is the teacher's responsibility to say things clearly and then follow through with action.

When Corinne and I met after this discouraging morning, she knew she had been ineffective with Hayley. She said something that left me feeling discouraged and concerned about ineffective teacher preparation. "If you had not been observing, I would have taken her off the structure, but I thought you would think I was being authoritarian!" The root of her comment is the common notion that being authoritative and direct is somehow being authoritarian. My work with teachers tells me this is a widespread challenge to our discipline. I agree with Lilian Katz that we need to work on accepting the authority that is ours. Children are left confused or, as in Hayley's case, at risk when we do not provide the adult supervision and directives necessary to keep them informed and safe.

> **It is the teacher's responsibility to say things clearly and then follow through with action.**

Here's an example of a teacher who accepts her authority with young children without being authoritarian or punitive. Laurie's room backs up to a field, woods, and then the community elementary school. This wonderful arrangement provides a safe and rich outdoor learning environment for her four-year-olds. Laurie is sensitive to young children's need for running and independence. Her particular location allows her to provide more of this than many of us are fortunate to have. She has an agreement with the elementary school to use its playground when the school's students are not outside. Laurie has mapped with photographs the route through the field and woods to the school. There are several big markers along the way—a huge rock, a fallen tree, a big stump, and so forth. Before her outings she goes over the map at group time and tells children they may run ahead until they get to the big stump. "When everyone reaches it, you may run to the huge rock," she says, reminding them that everyone needs a partner and no one may run ahead by themselves. She is very clear. They work independently *and* as a group as they reach each marker.

On the day I took this trip with them, Charlie broke the rules. He ran ahead by himself, though he stopped at the designated marker. When Laurie had the whole group together at the first marker, she said clearly, "Charlie, I'm disappointed that you did not stay with Trevor. Everyone *must* have a partner." Her tone and facial expression were sober. Her expectations were clear. She gave Charlie another chance but also stated the consequences, *in advance*, should he not stay with Trevor to the next marker. "If you do not stay with Trevor, I'll need to be your partner for the rest of the trip," she said. The race was on. The children took off, and once again Charlie left Trevor behind. At the huge rock, Laurie collected the group and took Charlie firmly by the hand. She didn't say a word. She announced the next marker, the children ran off and she kept Charlie firmly at her side. He squirmed, frowned, cried, and then accepted his fate. Laurie smiled at him and picked up her pace. They ran together laughing and racing. The few minutes of Charlie's struggle for independence he could not handle was a small price to pay for the assurance he felt as he ran with his teacher— the certainty that she would keep him safe and do what needed to be done. This is a wonderful gift that strong teachers give to the children in their care.

• • •

Behind Behavior: Four Factors

The way we talk to children in situations involving inappropriate behavior is an area in need of much discussion and clarification. This is complicated because the problem is multidimensional. In thinking about the problem of teachers' talk with children in behavior management situations, we have to consider these four pieces of the picture:

- Teachers
- Parents
- Culture
- Children

Teachers

Discussing discipline and young children is a delicate issue in the early childhood field. All one has to do is listen to teachers participating in a workshop on the topic to verify this. "I prefer *not* to say 'discipline'!" someone will say with passion. "It's so punitive! I prefer 'guidance'!" Heads will nod in approval, and teachers immediately zoom off on the topic of positive language, rephrasing the negative to give children an idea what *to* do instead of what not to do.

Though I used to encourage teachers years ago to find ways to phrase most of their directives to children in the positive, I have stopped. I think we've gone too far. We don't like to talk about it much, but all the while that teachers are saying they don't even want to say the word *discipline,* they are claiming behavior has never been more difficult. When children get nothing but sweet smiles and vague comments about not hitting our friends in child care, it's no wonder chaos reigns in many programs. I've been trying to empower teachers lately to give a good firm "*Stop!*" with a frown on their face when a child is about to hurt another. Recently a colleague shared another powerful deterrent with me: "Absolutely not!" a teacher might say with an "I mean business" look on her face. Don't be afraid to accept the authority that is yours. Find your voice so you can help children to find theirs!

Many textbooks offer us checklists on children's behavior aimed at assisting us in identifying our own weak points, sometimes referred to as *flash points*. We all have vulnerabilities to certain behaviors. Often it is connected to our own upbringing or early school years. These flash points are the things that make us really cringe when colleagues observing the same behavior have no problem at all. It may be whining, shouting, swearing, tattling, or hitting.

> **We don't like to talk about it much, but all the while that teachers are saying they don't even want to say the word *discipline*, they are claiming behavior has never been more difficult.**

We may not quite know why, but whenever this behavior surfaces in our classroom, our ability to cope feels diminished. This is absolutely normal, and common to all people who work with children. The important thing is to identify what your flash points are. When you know you have a vulnerability to whining, and you know Heather is a whiner, it's a good idea to let your assistant or colleague manage Heather on a day that you already have a headache. One of the most helpful solutions to this dilemma is teacher reflection. Margie Carter and Deb Curtis (1994) make the point that we go from task to task in our work, sometimes not taking the time to discuss how things went or *felt*. Reflection with colleagues can really be a support when dealing with children's difficult behaviors and our own difficult reactions to them.

Parents

In 1999, Rebecca New shared with teachers her experiences working with families in Italy in a lecture to Strafford County Head Start. In her experience the parent dimension in Italy is often not quite so complicated as it gets here because the culture is more homogeneous. Parents, teachers, and grandparents have greater agreement regarding what is good for children. Most teachers I talk to struggle with the fact that parents of the children they care for want very different things for their children. Some parents, teachers tell me, do not want their children corrected by anyone. These parents feel their children are too young to understand limits and will be stifled by teacher direction. In the same class are parents who arrive in September offering a wooden spoon and requesting that teachers use it on the child's legs if she misbehaves. Some parents don't want male children wearing dress-up clothes, some don't want their children to get their clothes dirty, and some want teachers to teach their three-year-olds to read. There are parents who expect you to prevent biting in a toddler room and parents who want you to bite a child back when he bites! So what is a teacher to do?

Years ago the answer to this question was always "Educate the parents!" We have learned a great deal over the years, and now most teachers agree it isn't quite that simple. As we have done more cross-discipline work, we have learned that we need to consider cultural and other differences between teachers and the families they work with such as nationality, ethnicity, socioeconomic status, and temperament (of teachers, children, and parents). Teachers' jobs are not so simple as educating parents in the right ways! In order to do right by children, teachers have to be as open to learning from the parents as we want them to be open to learning from us. Parental expectations differ as we move from one socioeconomic or cultural group to the next (Wardle 1999, 13), yet many teachers and programs don't modify their expectations or delivery to accommodate these differences. Addressing these issues can only enhance our ability to meet the needs of more children and create more peaceful classrooms.

Here are some examples of ethnocentrism often heard in early childhood settings:

- She's way too young to consider toilet teaching.
- It's time to get her on a bottle (*or* using a cup).
- He should be sleeping in his own bed.
- We need to get her to speak up when she needs something.
- That's not the kind of word people use.

Long ago most early educators abandoned expressions like *good girl*, *bad boy*, *stupid*, *naughty*, and so on. Less than a month ago, however, I overheard a teacher say, "That's a nasty word," in response to a four-year-old's use of the F word. Think about the unspoken judgment this phrase implies of a child's uncle, mother, or sibling who might use the F word frequently. A phrase like "That's a word we don't use at school" is more effective because it is not value-laden. It informs the child about the school rule without judging her family.

In addition, I still hear teachers discuss a child's out-of-control behavior using a phrase such as "She comes from a broken home, you know." Even most two-year-olds know what *broken* means. They know because they've seen a glass shatter on the floor. They know because they've seen things thrown out because they're broken. As part of professional training and behavior, it's important to remember these images and think before referring to any child's home as *broken*.

Gwen Morgan of Wheelock College (2001) has given us the thoughtful challenge of differentiating the things that are complex in our work from those that are complicated. The complicated can be simplified, but the complex can only be coped with. Morgan claims we have put misdirected energy into trying to simplify the complex, when our task is to develop coping strategies for complexity and ambiguity—for the many times in working with children and families when there is no "right" way.

Culture

Janet Gonzalez-Mena has given us much to think about regarding culture in her book *Multicultural Issues in Child Care* (1993). She reminds us that we have been fairly ethnocentric in North America in our approach to many developmental issues, such as feeding, weaning, toileting, and sleeping arrangements. As we ponder the many variables that make our work guiding the behavior of young children complex, we must consider culture. Many of us, particularly white middle-class women, feel uncomfortable approaching the topic of cultural differences. In her book *Other People's Children,* Lisa Delpit suggests that Caucasian, middle-class teachers who approach children of color and poverty in a soft wishy-washy manner cannot possibly gain the respect of these children, whose parents are likely to remain quite authoritarian in their parenting practices. Considering these powerful factors should have an impact on approaches we take in our daily work with children. Yet frequently we are judgmental regarding parenting practices that are different from ours, and both children and their parents know it. We need to broaden our definitions of guidance. Teachers who work with diverse children (in other words, all teachers) must be informed about and comfortable with a variety of approaches to discipline.

Carol was concerned about Sri's behavior during free play. She had recently come to this country from India and was living with her older brother and their parents in the motel they managed. It did not take long for Carol to realize that Sri was watching TV most of the time she spent at home. She came to school acting out kicks, punches, and wrestling that she saw on TV. Language was a barrier because Carol and Sri's parents had difficulty understanding each other. Carol decided to do a home visit because she felt uncertain as to whether Mom even knew what Carol was saying when she tried to show that Sri's kicks and punches were connected to watching television.

At the motel she was startled to find that the sister and brother were often alone in their room while Mom cleaned other guest rooms. This teacher was alarmed and wondered if it was appropriate. Sri's mom was able to explain that the room was safe and she was, after all, in the building. She did not see anything wrong with this arrangement. Carol decided to focus on the TV issue and sat with the parents, showing them the kind of behaviors Sri was modeling from the wrestling characters on TV. Since the parents were concerned with her increased activity (difficult when living in a small motel room), they were grateful for the connection made between TV programs and Sri's acting out. With the help of a family advocate, they were able to agree that Sri's mom would select appropriate choices (like *Mister Rogers' Neighborhood*) and then carry the controller to the TV with her as she cleaned rooms so her children could not change the channel to wrestling or cartoons. Over time Sri's behavior settled down.

Here are some of the things Carol learned from working with this family:

- Different families and cultures do not always share the same idea of what is "safe" space and supervision for young children.

- We need to learn more about the cultures of families new to our country and help them to learn more about ours.
- This work is very time-consuming and important, and it doesn't produce immediate results.
- While American educators tend to view TV as a deterrent to learning, many refugee and immigrant families view it as a language teacher.
- American teachers need to develop more skill at viewing scenarios from different angles.
- American teachers need to reflect on the extent to which we have been conditioned to be ethnocentric.

Here are two excellent references to assist teachers in multicultural learning: *A World of Difference,* by Carol Copple (Washington, D.C.: National Association for the Education of Young Children, 2003), and *Multicultural Issues in Child Care*, by Janet Gonzalez-Mena (Mountain View, Calif.: Mayfield, 1993).

Children

When we create a plan for classroom management, we need to begin with observation. As with curriculum, our approach to guiding behavior must be individualized. This creates distress in many teachers I know. Teachers love the word consistency, and nowhere is it more consistently applied than the area of child guidance. Yet children have different temperaments, personalities, and developmental needs. The same behavior does not necessarily mean the same thing when it is engaged in by different children. Teachers are the adults. Rules in a program need to be few but well maintained. Therefore a great rule for places where young children spend their days is "Listen to the adults in your room." That way the safety of the environment can be established by children understanding that we are there to support them and keep them safe. They can cope with adults having different interpretations of a rule. Children manage this at home with their parents, grandparents, and other adults. They can do it at school too. But they will be able to do it at school only when we develop a greater tolerance for ambivalence and more confidence making decisions on behalf of the children in our care. We need to continue to work on our inability to accept ambivalence as a natural part of responsible decision making. It is not always possible to feel completely comfortable with our decisions or course of action. But we must act.

Some of this hesitation comes from the extent to which positive guidance has been confused with permissiveness. Recently a teacher explained to me that in her classroom they were struggling with transitions and had set firmer limits around mealtime routines. It was only the third day of new routines when I visited the classroom. I sat next to a little boy who was told he needed to stay in his seat until his friends had finished eating. He had eaten quickly and wanted to return to a project, but the new routines included staying at the table until most of the children were done. He asked several times if he could get up. The teacher was struggling and finally said, "I'm so sorry I have to make you stay here, but it's the new rule."

After the children had gone, we talked about this incident. The teacher said she felt that she was being mean to the little boy. She said she wanted to let him do what he wanted to do because that was what she had learned in college about being responsive to young children. Most of us could agree that children behave better when we reduce waiting in our routines. However, for the child to have an apology from a teacher because she was carrying out a new plan for smoother mealtime routines does not help him to learn about life or waiting. More important, it doesn't help him trust that his teacher knows how to meet his needs with confidence.

How could this teacher have handled the situation positively? Knowing that the new rule required children to wait at the table until most of them were done eating, teachers in the room might have been prepared to help children with the task of waiting. Engaging children in interesting conversations or playing a game of *I Spy*, for instance, would have supported the children's learning of a new skill.

• • •

Teacher Talk and Behavior Guidance

So what does all of this mean when teachers are actually in the classroom with children? There is probably no situation in which clear "teacher talk" is more necessary than in the area of child guidance. Discipline situations require many things simultaneously from teachers:

- to move quickly
- to be fair
- to keep children safe physically and emotionally
- to teach everyone in the room, because they'll all be watching and listening
- to offer alternatives to inappropriate choices

To see how clear teacher talk can help with all of this, let's look at it in practice. Here's an example of a behavior guidance moment in a kindergarten classroom. Three boys were bouncing on a sofa that had been foolishly placed in front of a large window. The teacher clearly wanted this to stop but was ambivalent about how to get that to happen.

"I'm concerned that someone will be hurt," she said sweetly, with a pleasant smile on her face. Not surprisingly, the boys ignored her.

Her second attempt was a little stronger. "This looks dangerous to me," she said, not smiling. The boys continued to bounce.

Her third attempt sounded frustrated and angry. "You boys need to make other choices, *now!*" she said loudly. The boys, who were quite fond of this teacher, looked confused and hurt. They got down from the sofa and wandered around the room. They did not seem sure what they had done but were clearly affected by their teacher's displeasure.

After class the teacher talked with me about her frustration with the lack of discipline in her class. "The children don't listen to me. I don't know what to do," she said. We talked about the bouncing boys. She truly thought she had given them clear statements. We talked about the difference between an opinion ("I'm concerned") and a directive ("Please get down now. That's not safe").

We also talked about trying to match tone of voice, body language, and facial expression to the situation. It had not occurred to her that her smile and gentle tone prevented her concern from being heard. It is important that when we have a serious message to deliver to children, we do so in a serious tone of voice. Perhaps a frown is also in order. Safety is important. Children will not understand a serious warning if it is given in a gentle voice with a sweet smile. It is likewise important to shift gears once the dangerous behavior has ended. The above teacher could have given a firm directive followed by a softer voice, a smile, and a suggestion. "You boys need to bounce. Let's find the trampoline, and remember—sofas are for sitting!"

Let's think about the five components of behavior guidance as they affect this scenario of bouncing boys: ①moving quickly, being ② fair, keeping ③ children safe, teaching ④ everyone in the room, offering ⑤ alternatives. How could the teacher feel successful in such a situation considering all of these?

- She could have gone right to the sofa and assisted the boys in finding a safer place to bounce. She might have said, "Please get down now. This is not safe." (moving quickly, keeping children physically safe)
- She could use clear statements, use a firm tone of voice, and not smile when addressing unsafe behavior. (being fair)

- By putting an end to dangerous behavior in a fair way and by asserting her authority, she would provide clarity about what was acceptable and reassure children that she was strong enough to keep them safe. (teaching everyone, keeping children emotionally safe)
- She could have acknowledged the boys' need to bounce and found a way for it to be done safely. (offering alternatives)

Using Clear Language

Like other areas of teacher talk, our behavioral interventions with children are often directed by vague and uncertain words, fads, or poorly matched words and body language or tone of voice. Our best intentions combined with the above pitfalls result in our using expressions that baffle children completely and teach them little or nothing. Like poorly informed parents who shout, "Don't you ever hit," punctuating each word with a slap, teachers often say things like the following:

- "We don't hit (kick, bite, push) our friends in child care"—when somebody just did!
- "Tell her you're sorry. We don't hurt our friends"—when children are not sorry and they have hurt someone!

- "The sand needs to stay in the box"—as if sand had free will and is not being thrown by a person!

Teachers also often ask questions that don't clarify the situation but instead further confuse children who are already upset or put them on the spot. For example, here are a couple of questions that are not usually helpful:

- "Who had it first?" The response to this one is usually "I did!"—in unison! For children who are often still operating by the toddler's rules of possession ("If I saw it first, it's mine"), this question is irrelevant.
- "How would you like it if she did that to you?" Preschool-age children are not too young for empathy, but they are too young for a hypothetical situation like this one, especially when the reality is exactly the opposite. Better to state clearly the other child's feeling and help the offender tune in to visual cues about others' reactions: "That hurt Desmond. Look, he's crying."

The initial intent of such vague language was to prevent the kind of damaging words adults many years ago used with children. Avoiding name calling like *bad*, *nasty*, and *unkind* is a worthy and appropriate goal. But to say,

"We don't hit," right in the midst of hitting is confusing. "Stop. You're hurting Jesse!" helps a child to know what you want her to do and why. The third and critical piece of this kind of behavioral intervention is telling the child what *to do*.

1. "Stop." (what needs to be done)
2. "You're hurting Jessie." (why it needs to be done)
3. "Tell her you're still using the trike." (giving the child the actual alternative to pushing or hitting and the words to use as well)

It is important to remember that this kind of teaching involves continual repetition and patience. Helping children to learn self-control and social skills takes a very long time and much practice. When teachers respond to children's physical behaviors with each other in the same teaching way that they respond to other developmental milestones, children eventually learn the whole lesson we want them to learn: We can't hurt each other. We need to use words to get what we need and tell others how we feel. It is an exciting moment for a teacher who has said over and over again, "I can't let you hit. Hitting hurts. Use your words instead. Tell her to leave you alone," to watch a child, block in hand, ready to strike, consciously stop and say, "Go away. I want to be alone!"

Getting to that day, however, is a long journey. It takes patience, skill, and understanding. We need to develop empathy for the intense feelings young children have when they have not yet learned how to manage socially. In *Listen to the Children* (1986), these feelings are described perfectly:

> *Kevin and Greg are building blocks together.*
> *Kevin gets angry because Greg takes a block*
> *from him. They fight. The teacher intervenes*
> *and talks with Kevin about using words*
> *instead of fists. She tells him to try talking to*
> *Greg instead of hitting him—to tell Greg what*
> *was making him angry. Finally believing she*
> *has made her point, she asks Kevin, "Now*
> *what would you like to do?" Kevin answers*
> *without hesitation, "Hit him!" and he does!*

The teacher was hoping (as we so often do!) for the response "Say I'm sorry?" But note the language she used: "What would you like to do?" The child's response to this question was honest. Perhaps it was the wrong question—or perhaps what was needed at that point was not a question at all. We need to remember that heartfelt, sincere apologies in times of stress on a preschool floor are as likely as children stating, "This puzzle is beyond my developmental abilities," rather than pitching it angrily when they can't make the pieces fit. Haim Ginott (1965) was among the first to say out loud that when adults coerce an apology from a young child, they are, indeed, teaching them to tell their first lies! Young children push, hit, and grab at each other because they are still learning to get what they need and want. Their language skills are rudimentary. They have strong feelings. When their passionate needs are thwarted by us or a peer, they experience intense anger and don't yet know what to do with it. When they lash out, they are doing what they need and want to do at this point in their development. They are not sorry and shouldn't be asked to tell someone that they are.

So what can you do instead when you want children to transition from using their bodies to using their words? You can use *your* words. You can describe and define and repeat and understand.

So what can you do instead when you want children to transition from using their bodies to using their words? You can use *your* words. You can describe and define and repeat and understand. You can say, "You wanted the horse that Jenny had. When you grabbed it from her, it hit her in the eye. She's crying because it hurt. Let's get some ice to help her eye feel better."

Here's another example. This time, you are helping the children develop the concept of personal space. When one toddler pushes another, you might say, ("Zachary, Madison is showing me she doesn't want a hug right now. Madison, tell Zachary you want to be alone.") Or ("Zachary, I think Madison doesn't like you sitting so close. If you sit here, she will have more space.") The typical response, "We don't push our friends," doesn't give either child any idea what the problem is or what might be done about it. Indeed, it makes normal social interactions more confusing than they already are to children who are just learning how to be with one another in groups.

It is true that, in recent years, teachers report more and more behavioral challenges with children. In many situations teachers are unable to alter children's out-of-control behaviors. There are times when a child needs a one-on-one aide and times when a change of program is the only choice. But in the day-to-day world of teaching, your choice of words, tone of voice, and delivery really can make a difference. There are many elements involved in effectively using language to intervene in behavioral situations. Here are some basic guidelines:

- Match your tone of voice and facial expression to the situation.
- If you mean no, say "No!" or "Stop!"

- Avoid vague and wishy-washy requests when you need an immediate response.
- Tell the child what she can do instead of the unacceptable behavior.
- When the inappropriate behavior has stopped, soften your facial expression and support the child in moving to successful alternatives.

• • •

Discussion Questions

 1. What do you think Lilian Katz means by the statement that adults must accept the authority that is theirs due to knowledge, experience, and wisdom? Can you give some examples from your own experience? When do you find this easy or difficult?

 2. What is Gwen Morgan suggesting by differentiating between complicated and complex? Make a list of what is complicated and what is complex in your own work with children and families.

 3. Lisa Delpit suggests that white middle-class women feel uncomfortable dealing with class and cultural differences. Do you agree with her? Why or why not? Cite some examples from your work with children and families.

References

- Carter, Margie, and Deb Curtis. 1994. *Training teachers: A harvest of theory and practice*. St. Paul: Redleaf.
- Copple, Carol. 2003. *A world of difference*. Washington, D.C.: National Association for the Education of Young Children.
- Delpit, Lisa. 1995. *Other people's children: Cultural conflict in the classroom*. New York: New Press.
- Ginott, Haim. 1965. *Between parent and child: New solutions to old problems*. New York: Avon.
- Gonzalez-Mena, Janet. 1993. *Multicultural issues in child care*. Mountainview, Calif.: Mayfield.
- Katz, Lilian G. 1977. What is basic to young children? *Childhood Education*. October: 18.
- Morgan, Gwen. 2001. Personal communication.
- New, Rebecca. 1999. Lecture presented to Strafford County Head Start. Farmington, N.H.
- Wardle, F. 1999. Diversity means everybody. *Children and Families* 18 (2):13. Reprinted in A world of difference. *Young Children* (NAEYC, 2001):33.
- Zavitkovsky, Docia, Katherine Read Baker, et al. 1986. *Listen to the children*. Washington, D.C.: National Association for the Education of Young Children.

Chapter 4

Developing Skills and Concepts

. . .

f we wish to give the children in our care every learning advantage possible, we need to become comfortable with fostering a variety of approaches to learning. This might involve broadening our view of how children learn. Here's a list of the most common learning opportunities for children:

- Play
- Watching others
- Experiences
- Experimenting
- Doing
- Ideas from peers
- Imitating peers

- Mistakes
- Adults (conversations, modeling, systematic instruction)

The last example should motivate us to look more carefully at the role of teachers in extending children's learning. On the surface it seems such a simple thing and one to which most of us would respond, "Well, of course!" My observations of teachers and examination of conscience tell me that we are not as good at this as we like to think.

While some children seem to acquire a range of skills without systematic instruction, most children benefit from individualized instruction and assistance with building specific skills. Katz and Chard (1989) suggest that in recent years many teachers of young children have taken a hands-off approach to skill building because they confuse *systematic instruction* (teaching individual children a progression of skills that contribute to greater proficiency) with *direct instruction* (teaching the same skills at the same time in the same way to a whole class).

> While some children seem to acquire a range of skills without systematic instruction, most children benefit from individualized instruction and assistance with building specific skills.

Wanting to provide developmentally appropriate environments, teachers of young children shy away from direct instruction, or sitting a group of children down for instructions at the same time. However, teachers often fail to give children individual instruction in basic skills they need to get through the day. We can do a better job with this.

Tina attended a workshop about the importance of early literacy for later school success. She was worried about the children she served in her preschool room who would attend public school kindergarten in the fall. She was very aware that most of her students did not know letters or sounds and that many of their peers would be way ahead of them when they started school. She took some of the ideas from her workshop and developed a "word wall." She made a conscious effort to put the alphabet letters all over her room.

She had always worked on children getting to know the letter that begins their name but now expanded her morning group time to help children learn initial letters of other people's names and other words beginning with that sound. She put the new words up on the word wall. She dramatically sounded out words, stressing initial consonant sounds. She was certain that her four-year-olds were now getting a better preparation for kindergarten.

The day I visited her, however, it was her three-year-olds she asked about.

Tina had always had the policy that group time was mandatory for all of the children. We had discussed it many times. I've always thought it too much of a challenge to find an appropriate group time to meet the needs of very young threes, very old fours, and everyone in between. So Tina and I had often discussed a variety of approaches to this topic. This particular day she was feeling discouraged that her threes were suddenly acting out and making group time difficult for everyone. As we talked, it became clear that the behavior issues had begun about the same time she initiated her expanded "early literacy" work at group time. We talked about the need for fours to work harder on these skills. I also suggested that initial consonant sounds don't thrill three-year-olds too much and maybe there was a connection here. Tina and I listed the factors we both considered to be part of the dilemma:

- Tina thought she was providing her fours with necessary systematic instruction but was indeed giving a mixed-age group direct instruction in what was a poor developmental match for her young threes.
- Although the children are naturally interested in the letters of their own names, the "word wall"

concept and initial consonant work took literacy out of a meaningful context for fours and was completely inappropriate for her threes.

- Lack of interest in what was going on made the three-year-olds find other ways to amuse and interest themselves!

- Tina's enthusiasm for early literacy activities needed to be more individualized and matched to the children whose skill level was ready to take that leap.

- Tina could find ways to provide letter recognition or initial sound work in ways that were more developmentally appropriate and also in a more meaningful context.

It was a leap for Tina to decide that her work with her four-year-olds needed to be done at a different time from large group time. She worked on finding short, wonderfully illustrated alphabet books to share during group instead. She found some new alphabet songs and limited those two activities to the whole group. Next she worked on developing a more sophisticated writing area that was an immediate draw to the children who were both ready and interested in doing serious writing. Little by little, as Tina was able to share the joy of her older students who started writing and reading their own books, she was able to spend her group time in a more suitable way for *all* of the children.

Robin had a different approach to working with her four-year-olds. She carefully observed her children during free play times and then used those notes to guide her planning for the following week. Much of her curriculum was emergent. The emergent interests of children often resulted in wonderful and rich project work. For example, Chris, the assistant teacher, was building a new house. The children went to the construction site to watch. Tools, hard hats, and hammering were soon filling the preschool room. As the children read books about building, took photographs of different kinds of buildings, and brought in pictures of their own homes, the interest heightened. The children started paying more attention to their own school building.

Robin was quick to catch the spirit of their inquiry and surprised to realize how little they had explored this environment where they gathered every day. She carefully orchestrated an in-depth study that touched on math, literacy, science, and creative arts. The children graphed the different materials in their building. They did crayon rubbings of bricks, boards, and cinder blocks. They mapped the plumbing through their building and watched a plumber replace the wax seal of a toilet in their bathroom. They designed "blueprints" and built structures.

They wrote books about their study. Robin had never done a great deal in her woodworking area. Suddenly she found herself taking very seriously the need for direct instruction to the children regarding use of tools, safety goggles, and directions for building bookcases! Notice the extent to which the children's interests guided Robin's instructions and curriculum. The learning throughout this project was deepened because of the meaningful context in which it unfolded.

. . .

Respond to Classroom Conversations

When you ask most teachers or parents what the role of a preschool teacher is, the majority will answer that it is to help children get along with other children and to learn the things they need to know before going to school. If asked for clarification, the same groups would say, "You know—how to share, get along, follow directions, and know their colors, shapes, and alphabet."

As a supervisor of student teachers for many years, I have repeatedly heard students complain that I always managed to observe their program during transitions or mealtimes rather than their group time. Many teachers who are new to the field believe that the real learning goes on when they are front and center with a book or flannelboard activity to share with the children. Too often curriculum is evaluated as successful in terms of whether the children enjoyed the activity. However, every day we have opportunities to deepen and extend children's learning and understanding of their world. Too often we don't acknowledge or act on these opportunities.

R. F. Dearden (1984) outlined four criteria for curriculum relevance that can be used to evaluate the kinds of learning opportunities we share with children:

1. immediate applicability of the topic to children's daily lives
2. contribution to a balanced school curriculum
3. value in preparing children for later life
4. advantage of learning about this in school as opposed to another setting

Katz and Chard (1989) expand on these ideas by suggesting that children's learning must relate to the demands society will make on them.

I don't want to discourage teachers from engaging in dinosaur projects or Backwards Clothes Days. Fun is important for all of us. It reduces stress and nurtures awareness in children that playfulness is essential to a well-lived life. However, to consider these projects to be well-planned learning while disregarding the responsibility of clarifying misinformation about prisons, weapons, poverty, or skin color is to miss an important piece of our goal as teachers: To assist children to better understand and function in the world we live in.

Often teachers are reluctant to address difficult issues with children. It's easy to forget that children will make meaning out of what they experience, with our help or without it. Isn't it better to help them if we can? Here's an example of an issue that surfaced in a Head Start classroom I observed, in which the teacher was leading a seemingly innocuous group time about community helpers.

The teacher told the children that Officer Friendly would be visiting to share with the children the many ways that their community police helped people in trouble. Joshua leaned over to Carlos and said, "My dad says they are all fucking pigs." The teacher told Josh that the F word "is not a word we use here." She did not address the meaning behind what he said, where this idea might have come from, or the effects of his words on other children in the circle. I continued to observe and heard children talk about "cops" in dramatic play. I saw an "arrest" as well done as any on the TV program *CSI*!

I heard one child say, "They aren't friendly. They take you to jail."

A less sophisticated member of the group said, "What's jail?"

A peer quickly chimed in, "It's where the bad guys go!"

Two of the children in this class of seventeen had incarcerated parents. It is a scary thing to address hard and sensitive issues with children, or even with one another. But when we work with young children we have a responsibility to do so.

When the children had gone, the teacher and I sat down and talked about the day. I asked what she was thinking when she heard the passionate conversations going on in dramatic play. She said she was sad because she knew some of the children had parents in jail. She said they must have felt bad when other children said, "That's where the bad people go."

"Could you have done anything to help?" I asked.

"I didn't want to get in the middle of it," she said honestly. "What if I said the wrong thing? It was like a can of worms I didn't want to open!"

I didn't blame her for being hesitant. At the same time, with so much at stake in the lives of young children, teachers can't afford to be afraid of opening a can of worms. It is true that we need to choose words very, very carefully. But it is possible to address children's burning concerns in a way that makes room for all the children's experiences. Teachers can begin by asking questions like

"Why do you think so?" or "What do you know about that?" They can acknowledge children's strong feelings with phrases like "Sounds like you really miss your dad," or "Sounds like your dad was really angry at the police." Ultimately, teachers can also frame the different views of the situation for all the children in the room by giving information, saying something like, "All people make mistakes. Sometimes we can learn from them. We need to try to make it right when we do something wrong. When people are in jail, they are trying to make it right for the mistakes they have made." This explanation benefits all of the children in the class. But for the children whose family members are incarcerated, it is essential.

Teachers can't afford to be afraid of opening a can of worms. It is true that we need to choose words very, very carefully. But it is possible to address children's burning concerns in a way that makes room for all the children's experiences.

Here's another example of a time when seemingly innocuous curriculum strayed into deeper waters and a teacher took on the challenge of addressing difficult issues with children. Stacey was planning curriculum around new babies and being an older sibling, since both Evan and Sara were expecting new babies at their houses.

The work began with lots of new babies to "wash" in the water table and an array of wonderful children's books about new babies. The children had helped their teacher plan a party for Evan and Sara. The school got them "I'm the Big Brother/Sister" T-shirts, and the children brought in tiny gifts for the new babies at Evan's and Sara's houses.

The light nature of this curriculum changed when three of the girls got into an in-depth discussion of how the whole "baby thing" actually happened. Stacey observed Becky and Sara playing "pregnant." Baby dolls under their shirts were to be delivered by Dinah, the doctor. Becky insisted that babies get taken "out of your belly." With exasperation, Sara informed her she had her facts all wrong. "Babies come out of your vagina," she insisted, loudly. "And nobody takes them out—they come when they're ready!"

Stacey was a little nervous but proceeded to talk with parents about the children's interest in where babies came from. Jon's mom told them about her cesarean section, pleasing Becky, who was proved correct—some babies do get taken out of people's bellies! The curriculum took a leap from celebration to information, and before the year was over all of the children knew a great deal more about real human life cycles.

· · ·
Teach Basic Skills

Teachers help children learn with the environments they create, the experiences they provide, the
conversations they engage in, the questions they ask, and
the encouragement they give children to think for themselves. Good teachers also support children's learning by
teaching them important concepts and assisting them in
developing essential skills. Here are some essential skills
young children are learning:

- Self-help skills (buttoning, zippering, tying)
- Using glue and scissors
- Using eating utensils
- Pumping a swing
- Pedaling a tricycle
- Washing hands and brushing teeth
- Taking turns
- Expressing their own wants and needs
- Understanding others' wants and needs
- Negotiating conflict
- Solving problems

Children will not develop these skills without systematic instruction from parents and teachers. We need to
provide children with facts and tools and with the knowl-

edge of how to use these facts and tools to discover more about the world around them. This is very different from giving an entire class, ready or not, direct instruction on how to write a poem, hold a pencil, or zip a zipper.

Throughout the day children present teachers with many, many opportunities to teach, to make meaning, and, yes, to correct their unclear or incorrect understanding of real-world objects and ideas. Often teachers forget that free play is an excellent time to make the most of individualizing learning for young children.

Psychologist Kathleen McCartney (1984) provides us with evidence that children truly need intentional efforts on the part of teachers to help them develop language skills and ideas. Children simply chatting with each other as they play do not provide each other with adequate stimulation or enough meaning to polish their intellectual skills. McCartney's study randomly selected children from seven child care centers (of varying quality) where verbal interactions were observed and recorded. Children were later evaluated on several language and cognitive scales. Her results indicated that the quality of the child care environment and the amount of verbal interaction between children and adults were clear predictors of how children scored on cognitive and language measures. The study measured not only the amount but also the kind of verbal interaction. High-scoring children had teachers who used fewer controlling and more information-giving conversations with children.

Teachers sometimes hesitate to provide information to children because they have been cautioned against dominating the day with teacher talk. While it is true that we want to listen to children and encourage their language, it is also true that we need to model language and teach concepts as children question possibilities during block and water play. Teaching facts supports children's learning. Teaching thinking and reasoning supports children's learning. Their use and purposes are different, but both are essential in nurturing language and intellectual development.

Facts are helpful to children. Expanding a child's vocabulary of simple concept words (hard, soft, wet, dry, hot, cold, and so forth) helps the child to make accurate descriptions or repeat information correctly. By learning facts children become more competent at describing, listening, repeating, recalling, and following directions.

Teaching facts supports children's learning. Teaching thinking and reasoning supports children's learning. Their use and purposes are different, but both are essential in nurturing language and intellectual development.

The higher-level skills required for divergent thinking (or, thinking that leads to many options and possibilities; see page 100 for further discussion) and mental reasoning call on children's advanced cognitive development as well as on teachers' skills at questioning and nurturing creative solutions. It is also an important role of the teacher to extend and correct information that surfaces as children test ideas and even stereotypes during their dramatic play.

So what can teachers do about all of this? The first step is to respond to children's questions and statements in the classroom and to engage children in conversations during free play times. Here are some examples of children's statements I have heard in the last year during free play. All of these offered learning opportunities that teachers ignored.

- Dogs can't swim—just fish!
- Girls are the nurses.
- You can't put the little one under the big one—it won't work.
- Only girls wear the ballet shoes. Boys don't dance.
- If you mix the red and blue paint, you just get black.
- If it's bigger, it makes the scale go down.

All of these could use some careful questioning and clarification from the teacher. It is a teacher's responsibility to make meaning for children as well as to respect each child's family and values. This calls for thoughtful responses. We need to listen and think before we speak, but we must speak. If children have been arguing in dramatic play that Heather can't be the doctor because she is a girl, we need to listen to what has been said. Did Travis say his dad said girls are the nurses and boys are the doctors? The best approach may be a cautious one. For example, an attentive teacher might offer different information by saying something like "That's interesting, Travis. You know, my sister had a baby last week, and the doctor was a woman. I wonder how that happened."

It is helpful to children when teachers interject language that helps them to think things through for themselves. Here are some examples:

- What makes you think that?
- Could you try it and see what happens?
- Can you think of another way to do it?
- What do you know about this?
- What did you try?
- Why do you think that is so?
- Has anyone ever seen a (boy dancer, woman doctor, dog swimming)?

- Sometimes that's true, but I wonder what would happen if . . .
- Has anyone taken their dog to the beach? What happened?

Another way of correcting uninformed facts we hear from children is to conduct an experiment. Test out the children's statements, and see if they are true or not. This is the basic scientific inquiry process. For example, I have often heard preschoolers say you can't grow vegetables inside because plants need dirt, water, and sun. How about an experiment to find out if you have to plant seeds outside in order for them to grow? Children are fascinated as they realize that the sun coming through the window works just like the sun outside, that if you don't water your plant it really will die, and the important life lesson that sometimes you do everything you were supposed to and the plant still dies. The lessons are many! The lessons for teachers are many as well.

Let's go back to the preschool teacher reading *Green Eggs and Ham* at story time. Here's the story again:

"I'll begin the story when everyone is sitting nicely!" the teacher said.

The children continued to wiggle and squirm. The teacher became increasingly agitated. Finally her assistant said, "C'mon, kids, we need to crisscross apple-sauce here."

The teacher began reading *Green Eggs and Ham*. As usual, the children had comments right off the bat.

"There aren't really no green eggs."

"Are too, like you get in your Easter basket."

"Those aren't real eggs."

"Are too." (Louder.)

"No!" (Louder still.)

Here the teacher interrupted the discussion, say-ing, "Inside voices." The children ignored her, and her own inside voice got louder. "Inside voices!" she asserted loudly. "We need to get back to our story!" The children settled down again, but several of them were clearly still thinking about the question of green eggs and whether they really exist!

At the end of the story the teacher asked, "What happened?"

The children said in unison, "He liked the green eggs and ham."

The teacher beamed and said, "So you see we should always have a no-thank-you bite because we have to try things. We can't say we don't like something if we never tried it."

In Chapter 2 we talked about the vague directions the teacher gave the children when she wanted specific behaviors from them. But there is something else going on here too. The teacher focused on the children's behaviors using phrases like *inside voices*, *crisscross applesauce*, and *no-thank-you bites* instead of following up on the learning and experimental possibilities that had presented themselves. What might have happened if she had returned to the subject of real eggs and whether they are green? A difference of opinion is such a wonderful opportunity for learning. It's always tempting to end the conflict instead of clarifying the different ideas—what could this teacher have done instead?

- Children could have cracked open many eggs to see if any were green.
- The teacher could offer to bring in the kind of candy eggs one child had mentioned.
- Children could have dyed white eggs green.
- The teacher could have engaged the children in more in-depth conversation about eggs (green or otherwise) to let them experiment with words, ideas, concepts, and learning from each other. She might have asked questions like these:
  - What makes you so sure there are no green eggs?
  - Why do you think Jenny knows there are green eggs?
  - How and why do things change color?

It is always a challenge for teachers to know just when and how to respond to children's questions and challenges in the face of the teacher's own agenda. Here's a story that shows a teacher switching gears with finesse when a simple group time on "Our Families" led to discussions of hurt, anger, and divorce.

Glenda had read a story about families that was warm and pleasant, but not sugary. She followed up with talk about loving the people in our families. Four-year-old Henry didn't want to hear it. "Not me!" he shouted.

Glenda sweetly responded that sometimes we get mad at the people in our families, but we always love them.

"Not me!" Henry shouted more loudly and passionately.

"It sounds like you are really mad at someone in your family this morning," Glenda said, gently.

The flood gates were opened, and Henry cried that his dad yelled and left and now his mom was getting a divorce. "I hate them," he said.

Glenda was a bit relieved when Samantha said, "My dad left, and I don't hate him. He bought me my new bike."

"Families make us feel lots of things," Glenda said. She quickly reached for a book on feelings and read it with the children. When they were finished, she offered choices to children, including staying with her to draw or write stories about families and feelings. Many children moved on, but many stayed right there, talking about their own feelings when parents were angry or when children felt scared and sad.

What is important about Glenda's story is her recognition of Henry's immediate need. She also tactfully allowed children not needing to talk or interested in talking the opportunity to go elsewhere, but she was able to set aside her plans to do the real, important work of early educators: helping children to understand their world and all the wonderful and difficult things that includes!

Asking Questions

One of the best ways that teachers can stimulate children's thinking and learning is asking good questions. Making statements instead of asking questions can sometimes put an end to a discussion that offers great possibilities for children to learn from each other or from their own misinformation. As teachers, our repertoire of questions is always in need of expansion and practice.

The dictionary defines *question* as "an expression of inquiry that invites or calls for a reply; a subject open to controversy; an unsettled issue." When I think of questions frequently asked of young children in preschool, it's hard to find the controversy, the unsettled issue. Below are questions I hear frequently:

- What shape is this?
- What letter is this?

- Who is line leader today?
- Whose turn is it?
- Do you like pancakes?
- What is your favorite color?
- Did you hear me?

It is sad but somewhat true that many teachers still think part of teaching is getting children to give us the "right" answer. We are conditioned to ask questions to which we already know the answer. Children either sense our insincerity or sometimes are genuinely perplexed, like the boy who, when asked what color his shirt was, replied, "Wow, Teacher, you still don't know your colors!"

The purpose of a question is to get information that we don't already know. Remember that basic guideline—never ask a question to which you already know the answer. This applies to supporting children's learning as well as to guiding their behavior. Philosophers through the ages remind us that we learn more by looking for the answer to a question and not finding it than we do from learning the answer itself. If this is true, we certainly want to develop better skills for asking questions requiring a search or much discussion.

Judy believes children are never too young to be exposed to fine art. Her room has changing art exhibits of both child and adult art, still lifes, portraits, and fascinating prints of medieval paintings, complete with busy streets where vendors call and dogs bark. I am fascinated by the work she can introduce with a few simple questions. "Why do people paint?" she asked at group time one May morning. Here is what children said:

- "Because their moms don't let them at home!"
- "Because they like the way the colors look."
- "Because they want to remember something like a walk with their papa."
- "Because their car gets wrecked and needs the scratches gone."
- "Because they like the way the paint runs down the page when Cindy puts too much water in!"
- "Because their moms like it on the 'frigerator."
- "Because Grandma says the house should be a different color."
- "Because the teacher says it's your turn."

Judy wrote all of these reasons on a large poster board. Then she asked questions about each response:

- Why don't moms let you paint?
- What is it you like about the colors?
- How does the picture help you to remember?

- Do they paint the car with a brush? How does it happen?
- How is the paint different when there is too much water?
- Why do moms like pictures on the refrigerator?
- Why does Grandma want the house to look different?
- How is it different to paint when the teacher says it's your turn than when you just decide you want to paint?

I was fascinated at the depth of conversation that followed with Judy's five-year-olds.

When Judy does a project, it lasts for a long time. She showed children a huge variety of paintings, one day at a time, recording their thoughts and feelings about each one. Some were scary. Some were interesting. Some were just pretty, others *beautiful*! Each day she would ask: Why? and why? and why? in response to the children's comments. She had the children offering critique and explaining to peers why the painting made them sad, scared, interested. I was with her the day the children took a field trip to the Currier Gallery of Art. The adults at the museum were amazed that a group of children so young had such a high level of interest, asked so many interesting questions, and offered such sophisticated comment. It is not my intent to be simplistic. Much was involved in this long project. But I continue to believe that the course was set that first day when, instead of saying, "Today we are going to talk about painting," Judy began her group time with the question "Why do people paint?"

How can teachers develop these skills? The quick answer is to ask more *open-ended* questions (those that allow for multiple responses). Open-ended questions are associated with nurturing *divergent thinking* (producing many options or possibilities, which may result in unusual solutions), while *closed* questions (those requiring one correct answer) are associated with nurturing *convergent thinking* (putting all the pieces together to generate one solution).

Teachers develop convergent thinking skills by asking closed questions like these:

- Whose turn is it?
- Is it a fruit or a vegetable?
- How many legs does it have?
- Is it little or big?
- Where does it live?

Teachers develop divergent thinking skills by asking open-ended questions like these:

- What do you think?
- What would happen if . . . ?
- What else could you do?
- What could you do to fix it?
- How could you help her understand?

Even when teachers want to foster inquiry, they sometimes need simple yes and no answers to questions. For instance, if you are planning a field trip, it might be important to know who has been to the fire station, a car wash, or an ice cream factory and who has not. Clearly, if you are looking for a word that rhymes with cat, there are many correct answers, but *ball* is not one of them. There are certainly abundant reasons to ask questions that require a yes or no or right or wrong answer. As teachers, we also want to ensure abundant opportunities for children to think creatively, stretch their imaginations, and test their intuition. Open-ended questions help teachers do this. They also encourage children to talk more, which stretches their vocabulary and helps them get better at expressing themselves in words. That's what pre-literacy is all about!

Here are some guidelines to supporting young children's emerging thinking through teacher talk:

- Be sincere and authentic.
- Try to ask questions that nurture divergent thinking.

- Limit questions requiring yes or no answers.
- Increase your comfort level with not knowing the answer; join the children in searching for it.
- If you already know the answer, don't ask the question.
- Practice conversation starters like "What do you know about mice, Sammy?" rather than "Is this a mouse?"
- Start a conversation with "What do you know about this?"
- Welcome brainstorming ideas even with very young children.
- Validate children for suggesting solutions that couldn't possibly work!
- Acknowledge the importance of both content learning and critical thinking.
- Encourage fact finders with questions like "What did you see?" "How do you know?" "Does it have a name?"
- Encourage critical thinkers with questions like "Why do you think it melted?" "Why do you think this happened?" "What would happen if the wind didn't blow?"
- Observe children carefully and regularly to know which emerging skills to assist.
- Give children time to ponder.

Don't jump in too quickly to solve problems or offer accurate information. Wrong solutions offer great learning when active thinking is going on.

• • •

Discussion Questions

1. What skills and concepts do you hope to develop in the young children in your care? Pick one or two of the most important ones. How might you use teacher talk to help support children's development of these skills or concepts?

2. What do you think are some of the barriers to strong skill development? Is there anything that can be done to change these?

3. What do you think is the difference between "dispositions for learning" and actual skill development? Why are both important? What can you do to nurture both in the children you care for?

References

• Dearden, R. F. 1984. *Theory and practice in education.* London: Routledge & Kegan Paul.
• Katz, Lilian G., and Sylvia C. Chard. 1989. *Engaging children's minds: The project approach.* Norwood, N.J.: Ablex.
• McCartney, Kathleen. 1984. "Effect of quality day care environments on children's language development." *Developmental Psychology* 20 (2): 224–60.

Chapter 5

Conversations,
Discussions,
and Stories

• • •

research tells us that children who spend their time in conversation-rich environments become better speakers, readers, writers, and thinkers than their peers not exposed to effective use of language. Research also confirms that classrooms are dominated by teacher talk and that most of that talk takes the form of directives rather than invitations to verbal inquiry or complex discussion. We know that language is the key to all other kinds of content learning. Yet we often deny children the opportunity to question, disagree, conjecture, or play with language in a way that builds their communication skills and vocabulary.

Think for a minute about the times you have heard teachers say, "Listen," or "Be quiet, please," compared with the number of times you've heard teachers say, "What do you think?" or "Tell me all about it!" We are not doing the best we can at encouraging meaningful conversation.

Family time for meaningful conversation has also been reduced in recent years, because of the pace of life in this country and parental stresses of balancing work and family life. Research also indicates that the poorest of America's children fall way behind their middle-class peers in developing both vocabulary and language skills. One of the reasons for this is the lack of abundant and meaningful conversation. Clearly, language and literacy are both educational and class issues and therefore demand that teachers take very seriously their responsibility to create and model meaningful conversations in the classroom.

For any number of reasons, most adults are much better at talking *at* children than they are at talking *with* them. This is met with a number of responses from children. One response is to tune us out. Another is to slowly lose the wonder and passion for life that seem to accompany most children into the world. If adult response to children's excitement and discovery and their verbal attempts to share those is met with a distracted "Uh-huh," or "That's not what we are discussing, Taylor!" it is no wonder that, over time, they fall silent. They also respond by building rehearsed, dull, automatic answers to adults whom they perceive as not really interested.

Jim Greenman describes this perfectly in an article, "Just Wondering: Building Wonder into the Environment" (in Greenman 1993, 33). He tells us of his observation of unsought instruction as a mother and her four-year-old share a trip to the zoo:

> "Look, Johnny, flamingos!" the mother exclaimed. "What are they?"
> "Birds," said Johnny.
> "What color are they?"
> "Pink," said Johnny.
> "How many are there?"
> "Three," said Johnny.
> Two giraffes lumbered into view. Before Johnny's determined mom could open her mouth, Johnny called out: "Giraffes, yellow, two." Johnny had overdosed on teachable moments. Wonder comes from a child's search and discovery, not from our dutiful prodding.

Note, too, that Johnny's mother had disregarded one of the prime guidelines for conversations with young children: Never ask a question you know the answer to. Johnny's mom doubtless knew what kinds of animals she was looking at, what color they were, and how many there were.

Likewise, the wonder children bring to our classrooms can be snuffed out when we focus solely on our plan for children's learning rather than carefully listening to the children and following their conversational lead. This can be a real challenge, since we know young children speak from a pretty egocentric place: one child's response to a teacher's question about jungle animals gives birth to another child's discussion of his uncle's car.

Here's a conversation I observed in a preschool classroom. The teacher, talking about wild animals, asked the children if they knew names of any wild animals.

Juan immediately said, "Tiger."

This triggered some unsolicited conversation from Todd, who said, "My uncle's car is called Tiger. It's yellow, goes really, really fast, and my auntie says my uncle loves that car more than her!"

The teacher responded quickly, and typically, "We are talking about animals today, Todd, not cars."

For the rest of the jungle discussion, Todd was tuned out. He fidgeted, looked around, and didn't listen. He probably had hurt feelings as well as questions about what he had said to elicit such an uninterested response.

Todd probably offered too much information, but a connection could be made that would extend learning for all the children in the group. I am not suggesting the teacher involve the class in Todd's family relationships! But her response was disrespectful of Todd's participation. I wondered what would have happened had she said simply, "Why do you think he calls the car Tiger, Todd?" I didn't wonder about Todd's involvement with the rest of her circle time as much as what would have happened to this circle time discussion. Perhaps someone would have shouted, "Tigers are yellow," or "Tigers have stripes—does his car have stripes?" I can picture someone else saying, "Maybe because they both go really fast." Children would have conversed, questioned, come to conclusions. The teacher could have made connections and congratulated the children on their work. Todd would feel that he made a contribution. Instead he felt he'd done the wrong thing and wasn't even sure why.

> The wonder children bring to our classrooms can be snuffed out when we focus solely on our plan for children's learning rather than carefully listening to the children and following their conversational lead.

Here's another example. A teacher took her children to the woods to gather autumn leaves. When the children found a fallen tree covered with ants, they were amazed.

"Wow—there must be a million!"

"Are they born in the tree?"

"No! Man, they all climbed up there when it fell over!"

"How do you know?"

"Is he right, Teacher?"

Unfortunately, the teacher didn't address how the ants got there or where the children's guesses came from. "Come along, class," she said. "We are here to find leaves!"

Do teachers have to let go of their carefully laid plans and drift in any direction suggested by children's comments and questions? Of course not. Teachers are still the authorities in the classroom. We have a lot of knowledge and information that children want and need. But we can redirect our immediate plans and respond to children's emergent interests and conversations. We can find ways of addressing our concerns within the context of the children's interests and passions. Too often we allow ourselves to get caught in the pace of day-to-day life with children and not take the time to make interesting conversation with them or nurture it among them. We hurry from planned event to planned event without

> Teachers...
> We have a lot of knowledge and information that children want and need. But we can redirect our immediate plans and respond to children's emergent interests and conversations.

enough time to process what, why, or how we are doing what we do.

We have focused in earlier chapters on the effects of tone of voice and body language on our messages to children. Nowhere is this more noticeable than in the area of conversation. Children can tell when we are in a hurry. Developing strong conversational skills takes time. In addition to time, children need opportunities to think and ponder in order to learn. They need time to question and experiment. Yet frequently we prod children who are "doing nothing" into finding something constructive to do with themselves. Having thoughts, daydreaming, and pondering are constructive activities. We should provide opportunities for children to have chunks of time for solitude. Our observations of children should lead us to leave them alone now and again when we can see that they are deep in thought. It is always a balance. We want to encourage children to reflect, problem-solve, and converse, yet we don't want to interrupt, coerce, or distract them.

Alice Honig (2002) writes about the necessity of finding just the right tone of voice and thoughtful words to encourage a child to focus on problem solving without taking away her initiative. She also suggests that it poses an exhilarating challenge to early educators. I agree with Honig that it is an exciting challenge. In my experience, many teachers miss it because they are afraid to leave their own planning aside to get on board with spontaneous and interesting issues children present in their days with us. The demands of the future will not call on today's youngsters to remember information. Computers have memory. They will need to be able to make sense of information, manipulate it, organize it, and understand it to be successful in the world they will inhabit. Meaningful conversation and problem solving, research, and questioning will prepare children for this task.

I observed an interesting conversation recently between a teacher and a small group of children. Initially the teacher was asking questions because she did not understand what a child was asking her.

"Why were you outside?" Dante asked his teacher, Cindy.

"Do you mean at outdoor play?" Cindy asked.

"No! Why were you outside before?"

Dante came to this country when he was two. His mom still speaks very little English. Though he is learning quickly, many pieces of English still confuse him. This is true of most four-year-olds, but the language difference sometimes makes it even more confusing. It took Cindy a few minutes to register that Dante's question was one of these instances.

"Oh! You mean why was I not here yesterday?" Cindy asked.

Dante smiled and nodded.

"I went to help my mom yesterday."

"Why did he think you were outside?" Tanya asked.

"Because I wasn't here," Cindy said. "Dante knew I was someplace else, but he didn't know where I was and he wasn't quite sure how to ask the question."

"But if you weren't here yesterday, how could you have been outside?" Tanya pressed.

"Maybe because when I'm not in the room, at school, I am sometimes out on the play yard," Cindy proposed. "Why did you ask if I was outside, Dante?"

"Not here," Dante said.

Tanya looked at Dante, and then at Cindy. "I guess you're right!" she said.

Meaningful conversation can be a confusing thing for young children. They so often put a meaning on words or situations so much different from ours that it takes time and reflection to sort things through. Cindy made sense of a child's missing her and wondering where she was a day when she was absent. A less conscientious teacher might have dismissed this with "I wasn't outside," without getting to the meaning behind the child's words. Meaning is the key element when we have conversations with very young children.

The best way we can help children with this piece of development is by being meaning makers. Early on, I suggested that adults have a tendency to delight in the whimsical confusion of young children's experimentations with language. We chuckle. We repeat the stories. Sometimes we even write them down. But most of the time we do not clarify for children the error of their thought processes or provide more information that will help them to come to more appropriate conclusions on their own. This clarification is essential to help children make sense of the world. Below is a story in which the adults were too slow to pick up on the meaning and ideas in a child's mind to clarify for him words adults were using to describe his new baby brother.

The mother of one of the children in our Head Start program was about to give birth. Her son talked a great deal about the new baby coming. His teacher had read all the appropriate books. Children in the class had talked to him about babies at their house. It was wonderful to see his very experienced teacher let the conversations fly about babies smelling poopy all the time, yelling too loudly, forcing the dog to stay on the porch, and not being able to play with you anyway "'cause all they do is sleep and cry!" His mom finally delivered an almost ten-pound infant. The size of the baby was the center of conversations at the program in the morning.

"Wow, I heard he was huge!"

"I don't think I know anyone who has had one that big!"

"Colossal!"

I had the pleasure of lunching with the new big brother on the day his mom and new sibling came home from the hospital. I asked what he thought about all these exciting happenings at his house. "People kept saying he was huge. He fits in the apartment—no problem!" he said. It is clear that none of the adults had taken time to process with this little boy what ten pounds of new infant looks like. As I listened to him, I could tell the conversations he'd heard had him expecting something like Chuck E. Cheese or a huge float from a Macy's parade. The thing that interested me most about this was that all the adults loved the story. They talked about how "cute" it was. Someone suggested sending it to *Reader's Digest*! Teachers laughed and laughed. Yet I never heard anyone say, "Wow, that's pretty scary. Can you imagine what he was thinking? It's too bad none of us thought to clarify things for him."

> Most of the time we do not clarify for children the error of their thought processes or provide more information that will help them to come to more appropriate conclusions on their own.

The first step to doing a better job at conversing with children in a supportive way is to go back to our knowledge of child development and really think about the way a young child's thought processes are a work in progress. Reviewing the work of Jean Piaget might help with the developmental pieces. Or if that seems too arduous a task, find copies of Fred Gwynne's books *The King Who Rained* (1970) and *A Chocolate Moose for Dinner* (1976). Both are delightful reminders for grown-ups of how it sounds to a child when we say things like "Go to the fork in the road" or "Do you have a coat of arms?" or "We need more car pools in this community!" Another visual look at adult versus child understandings and conversations is the "Family Circus" comics by Bil Keane. One of my favorites shows a father and son walking in the snow. The snow comes up to the son's shoulders and the father's knees. The caption? You've probably guessed: "This is nothing! When I was your age we had snow that came right up to your shoulders!" As adults, it is true that we find these situations humorous, but as teachers of very young children, we need to remember that it is our job to urge children to question, explore, find out. It is also our responsibility to gently lead them to correct information to replace their misinformation.

Here are some guidelines that will help you talk *with* children rather than *at* them:

- Remember that children don't like being interrupted any more than we do!
- Get a child's attention by getting down to her
  level, calling her by name, and softly touching an
  arm or face as you speak.
- Model pleasant conversation for and with children.
- Really listen to children. Stop what you're doing.
  Establish eye contact. Stay focused. Respond
  encouragingly.
- Use expressions like these to encourage
  conversation:
    - "That's interesting."
    - "What happened next?"
    - "How could that be?"
    - "Does anybody else have an idea about that?"
    - "Did that ever happen to anyone else?"
- Make meals a place and time for conversation.
  Yes, manners are important, but it will take years
  for us to assist children in learning all the customs
  of class and culture. When a child shares an exciting story from her weekend with her mouth full,
  remember that encouraging conversation is just as
  valuable a goal as teaching manners. Encourage
  the conversation (see above) instead of saying,
  "Samantha, don't talk when your mouth is full."
- Establish a comfortable environment for adults
  and children to talk with each other. Provide both

adult- and child-sized furnishings in your class. Schedule chunks of time for children to have their own casual conversations. Ask engaging questions that get children talking. Bring interesting things into the classroom that the children do not likely know, and encourage them to guess the purposes, functions, and names. Think of other ways to encourage children's conversations in your classoom, and make it a place where everyone is talking!

. . .

Discussion Questions

 1. How can you handle children's developmentally appropriate yet seemingly random comments and interruptions in the middle of your group time or a focused discussion?

 2. List some ways to have meaningful conversations with children at mealtimes.

 3. How do culture, class, and other differences get in the way of children having rich conversations with one another and adults in their lives?

References

- Greenman, Jim. 1993. *Places for childhoods: Making quality happen in the real world*. Redmond, Wash.: Child Care Information Exchange.
- Healy, Jane M. 1992. *Is your bed still there when you close the door? and other playful ponderings: How to have intelligent and creative conversations with your kids*. New York: Doubleday.
- Honig, Alice. 2002. *Secure relationships: Nurturing infant/child attachment in early care settings*. Washington, D.C.: National Association for the Education of Young Children.
- Wharton-McDonald, Ruth. 2000. Lecture presented to Belknap-Merrimack Head Start, Concord, N.H.

Suggested Readings

• • •

Bodrova, Elena, and Deborah J. Leong. 1996. *Tools of the mind: The Vygotskian approach to early childhood education*. Englewood Cliffs, N.J.: Merrill.

Cazden, Courtney B., ed. 1981. *Language in early childhood education*. Revised edition. Washington, D.C.: National Association for the Education of Young Children.

Galambos, Jeanette W. 1978. *A guide to discipline*. Washington, D.C.: National Association for the Education of Young Children.

Gwynne, Fred. 1976. *A chocolate moose for dinner*. New York: Simon & Schuster.

Gwynne, Fred. 1970. *The king who rained*. New York: Windmill.

Schickedanz, Judith A. 1999. *Much more than the ABCs: The early stages of reading and writing*. Washington, D.C.: National Association for the Education of Young Children.

Szasz, Suzanne. 1978. *The unspoken language of children*. New York: Norton.

Zavitkovsky, Docia, Katherine Read Baker, et al. 1986. *Listen to the children*. Washington, D.C.: National Association for the Education of Young Children.